Raspberry Pi 4 Programming Made Simple For Beginners

A Comprehensive Guide On How To Setup and Work With The Latest Raspberry Pi 4 and Develop 20 Cool Raspberry Pi 4 Projects

Jack Berg

Raspberry Pi4 Made Easy

Copyright © 2020 Craig Berg.

This book is an independent publication and is not affiliated with, endorsed by, or sponsored by the Raspberry Pi Foundation or any of its affiliates. Raspberry Pi is a trademark of the Raspberry Pi Foundation.

All content in this book is original and based on publicly available information, research, and personal experience. While every effort has been made to ensure accuracy, the author and publisher do not guarantee the completeness or reliability of the information provided. Readers are encouraged to consult the official Raspberry Pi website or documentation for the most up-to-date and accurate information.

This book is for educational and informational purposes only. Any references to third-party products, trademarks, or materials are for illustrative purposes and do not imply any affiliation, sponsorship, or endorsement.

Unauthorized reproduction, distribution, or commercial use of this book or its content is prohibited without prior written consent from the author or publisher.

Introduction

"Nerd. One whose unbridled passion for something defines who they are as a person, without fear of other people's judgment."

Zachary Levi

If you are planning to acquire a Raspberry Pi, or if you own one but have no idea how to get started with it, you have come to the right place.

Welcome to this Raspberry Pi 4 guide, a comprehensive guide for beginners and intermediates with projects. This book will ensure that you fully understand, utilize, and, more importantly, enjoy your Raspberry Pi 4 to the fullest.

We will start by understanding the inner workings of the Raspberry Pi. Then, we shall move on to setting up a compatible OS for our Pi so that we can start coding and building robots and automated projects we can use to control smart devices. From there, we shall move on to experimenting with all kinds of weird and cool projects.

The Raspberry Pi has played a revolutionary role in making computing technology accessible and affordable to everyone.

People of all ages and gender are using this amazing device to create innovations that have the potential to improve the future.

If you're ready to use your Pi 4 to play your part, this a book will certainly help you.

Raspberry Pi4 Made Easy

Table of Content

Introduction _____ 2

Section 1 _____ 10

Getting Started with the Raspberry Pi 4 __ 10

The Raspberry Pi Hardware _____ 13

Hardware Specifics for the Raspberry Pi 4 _____ 17

Section 2 _____ 23

Setting Up the Raspberry Pi 4 _____ 23

Setting Up The Raspberry Pi Hardware _____ 29

Section 3 _____ 43

Installing Raspberry Pi Software _____ 43

How to Flash NOOBS to SD Card (Project #1)   44

How to Set Up NOOBS on Linux (Project #2)_ 52

How to Install Raspbian OS_____ 58

Section 4 — 63

Working With Raspbian OS — 63

How to Set up the Raspberry Pi 4 Using the Wizard — 64

How to Navigate The Raspbian Desktop (Like a Pro) — 66

Section 5 — 68

Installing Software — 68

Working With The Raspberry Pi 4 Command Line — 69

Linux Terminal Basics — 70

How to Set Up a Static IP (Project #3) — 71

Section 6 — 75

Connecting the Raspberry Pi Remotely — 75

Virtual Network Computing (Project #4) — 75

How to Connect to The Raspberry Pi Remotely Via SSH _____ 78

Section 7 _____ 80

Configuring the Raspberry Pi _____ 80

How to Set up the Configuration File _____ 80

Configuration Settings _____ 82

Section 8 _____ 96

Raspberry Pi 4 Projects _____ 96

How to Install Python 3 On the Raspberry Pi 4 (Project #5) _____ 98

C++ Installation (Project #6) _____ 99

NGINX Webserver (Project #7) _____ 100

Raspberry Pi Wi-Fi Extender (Project #8) _____ 103

Nagios System Monitor (Project #9) _____ 108

Mozilla WebThings (Project #10) _____ 114

Raspberry Pi Proxy Server (Project #11) _____ 118

Raspberry Mathematica (Project #12) _____ 122

Raspberry Pi Radio Station (Project #13) ____ 124

Setting Up Raspberry Pi for Penetration Testing (Project #14) _____ 134

Raspberry KODI Media Center (Project #15) _137

Raspberry Pi Torrenting With Deluge (Project #16) _____ 141

Raspberry Pi Google Assistant (Project #17) ___145

Raspberry Pi FTP Server (Project #18)_____156

Setting Up a Data Science Environment (project #19) _____ 158

Running a Flask Server On The Raspberry Pi (Project #20)_____ 160

#Bonus Project: Installing Kismet On the Raspberry Pi _____ 163

Conclusion _____ **167**

Section 1

Getting Started with the Raspberry Pi 4

"A computer is like a mischievous genie: it will give you exactly what you ask for, but not always what you want."

Joe Sondow

The Raspberry Pi is a fully functioning computer that comes in a tiny package and a very affordable price —while prices vary based on computing power, the basic Pi 4 starts at $35.

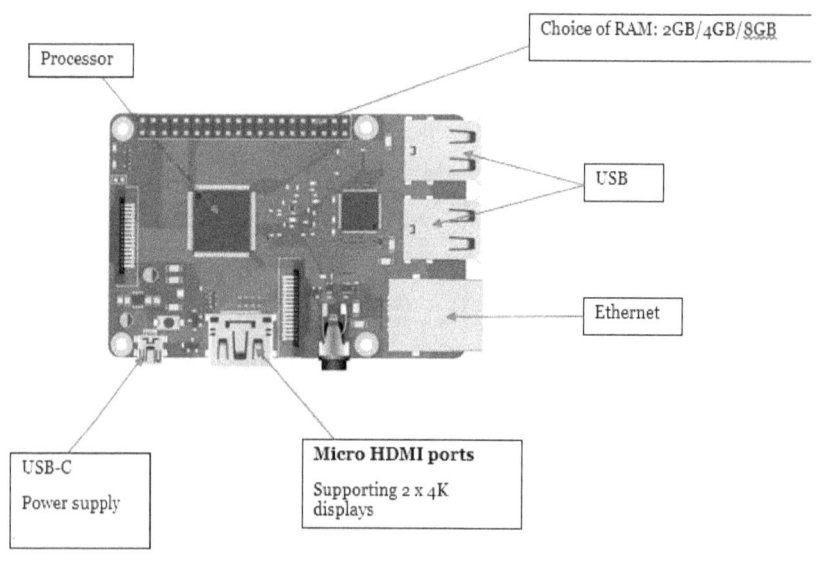

[1]Figure 1 Image Credit Shutterstock

Raspberry Pi4 Made Easy

From $35
You'll recognize the price along with the basic shape and size, so you can simply drop your new Raspberry Pi into your old projects for an upgrade: and as always. We've kept all our software backwards- compatible, so what you create on a Raspberry Pi 4 will work on any older models you own too

Whether you want a device that you can use to perform day-to-day computing tasks such as creating amazing programs, circuitry, or controlling other physical devices, the Raspberry Pi will adapt to whatever you need.

The Raspberry Pi brand is a full-fledged series of single-board microcomputers developed and maintained by the Raspberry Foundation.

Since its first development in 2012, the Raspberry Pi features have advanced drastically over the years. Today, it has illustrious capabilities and peripherals.

Since the initial release of the first Pi, the Raspberry Foundation has continued to release newer models, with newer models of the Pi supporting new features and capabilities.

The Raspberry foundation notes that today, they —and third parties— have sold more than 25 million Raspberry Pi kits all over the world, many of which have found use in classrooms, offices, factories, data centers, and homes where hardcore geeks use them for all sorts of things.

The Raspberry Pi is a single-board computer. That means its similar to a desktop, laptop, or smartphone but in a single circuit board.

Like most single board computers, the Raspberry Pi is simple and small, often the size of a credit card. However, the device's small size does not mean it's less powerful than other desktop computers. In some use case scenarios, the Raspberry Pi can perform a task better than larger desktop computers.

Despite the improvements made on each new model of the Pi year after year, all Raspberry Pis still have one main thing in common: *they are all backward compatible.*

Backward compatibility means that programs and projects designed on older models of Pi will work on newer models and vice versa.

You can even run a newer version of the Raspbian OS on the very first model of the Pi. It will run slowly, but it will still run.

NOTE: The above notwithstanding, throughout this book, we will be using the Raspberry Pi 4 for illustrations. However, thanks to backward compatibility, the projects and concepts we shall discuss will work with other models of the Pi. Where you may experience compatibility issues, we shall present an alternative you can use.

The Raspberry Pi Hardware

Unlike large desktop computers that hide all the inner hardware components, the Raspberry Pi has every component exposed to the user, which allows easy modifications and troubleshooting. This 'nakedness' also allows you to learn about core hardware components and how they work. It also allows you to manage any peripheral devices you connect to the Pi.

NOTE: If you wish, you can purchase a case to protect the Raspberry Pi, which is often better, especially since you can purchase a clear case.

The figure below shows the Raspberry Pi 4 from a bird's eye view. If you have another model, your Pi might look slightly different. Do not worry; we will discuss what the various parts entail and how they work.

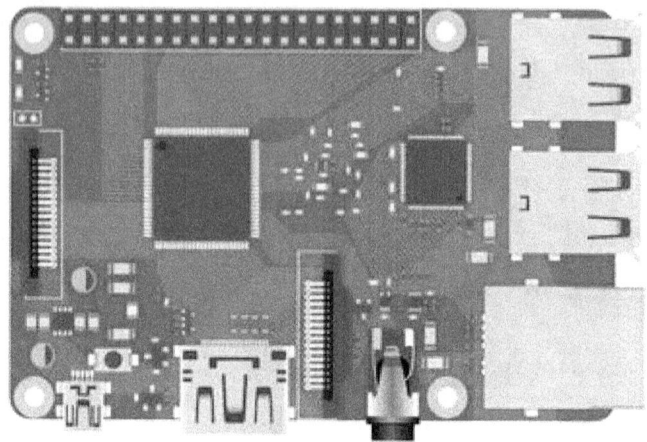

[2]**Figure 2 Image Credit Shutterstock**

Although the Raspberry Pi may seem to pack a lot of components into a single board, the parts are very simple and easy-to-understand.

Like most computers, the Raspberry Pi has particular components that play specific roles and help the Raspberry Pi function.

We will start by looking at what we can term as the most important part of the Raspberry Pi located at the center of the board covered in a metal cap: *the System-on-Chip or SoC*.

#: The Raspberry Pi 4 CPU

Although significant changes have happened with each new release of the Raspberry Pi, all models feature a Broadcom System on Chip (SoC) with an ARM-compatible CPU. The Pi has a clock speed range of 700 MHz to 1.5 GHz on the Raspberry Pi 4.

The Raspberry Pi 4 has a quad-core ARM Cortex-A72 processor, which is a successor to the Raspberry Pi 3 B+ processor quad-core Broadcom BCM2837BO that had a clock speed of 1.4GHz.

Raspberry Pi processors support overclocking at boot by running the command sudo raspi-config during the boot process on Raspbian Linux based distributions. Most of these processors are overclock-able up to 800MHz, 1000 MHz, and 1500 MHz on the extreme.

#: Raspberry Pi Memory

The Raspberry Pi Foundation has done a great job of improving the device's memory. Older models of the device featured 128MB allocated for the GPU, with another 128MB allocated to the CPU. The GPU in the Raspberry Pi is the

Broadcom Video-core VI. The Raspberry Pi 4 comes in flavors of 1GB, 2GB, and 4GB.

#: *Raspberry Pi Networking*

Older models of the Raspberry Pi have no ethernet connectivity, and the only way to connect them to the internet is by using an external USB ethernet or a USB wireless adapter.

Newer models such as the Raspberry Pi B and B+ support gigabit ethernet and use it as the primary connectivity interface.

Later models of the Raspberry like the Raspberry Pi 4 also feature an 802.11ac wireless interface and a BLE 5.0 Bluetooth support. The Pi 4 also has Gigabit ethernet.

#: *Raspberry Pi Storage*

The default storage for the Raspberry Pi is a micro SD card. This SD card is what you will use to install the Operating system and as the default storage disk—however, the Raspberry Pi 4 supports external storage devices via USB ports.

Those are the main features of the general Raspberry Pi. We left out some features that are specific to the Raspberry Pi 4 —and not the entire Raspberry family. We shall now cover those:

Hardware Specifics for the Raspberry Pi 4

As discussed, the Raspberry Pi is a British-built, low-cost single-board computer that gives everyone the ability to learn computing, hacking, and programming with a lot of ease.

The Raspberry Pi 4 is a small device whose size is similar to that of a credit card or driver's license. However, unlike a regular credit card, the Raspberry Pi is a full-fledged computer that can run full-stack operating systems.

Because of its flexibility, the Pi 4 gives you the ability to customize it by choosing an operating system of choice and the applications running on the device.

Setting up the Raspberry Pi is simple but can seem daunting to complete beginners. In this book, we will cover the entire set up of the Raspberry Pi, starting from the unboxing to using it to hack other systems.

Below is an image of the Raspberry Pi 4 with the exclusive features pointed out below.

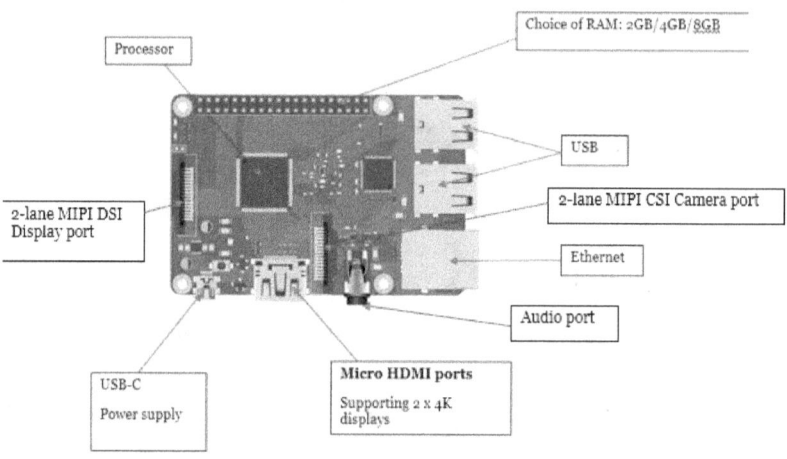

[3]Figure 3 Image Credit Shutterstock

Here are the purposes of each of these features:

#: The 40 Pin General Purpose Input/output (GPIO) header

The GPIO header connects projects with electric devices. You can access them directly on the Raspberry Pi.

NOTE: You can turn some Pins on or off while your Pi is still running —or in operation.

#: PoE Header

Power Over Ethernet (PoE) allows the device, once networked, to become capable of being automatically turned on/off at specific times.

Raspberry Pi 4 features the 4-PIN header that supports the PoE HAT released on the previous model of Raspberry Pi 3B+

#: Gigabit Ethernet

The Gigabit Ethernet hard-built into the Raspberry Pi 4 features a bandwidth speed of over 350Mbps.

Although this may not be as powerful as the regular desktop, it is a significant improvement over the Pi 3B+ that featured a gigabit Ethernet over USB 2.0 at 300Mbps. The Ethernet improvements add to the Raspberry Pi 4 feature-rich arsenal.

#: USB

The Raspberry Pi 4 has 4 USB ports. 2 USB 2.0 ports and 2 USB 3.0 ports indicated by blue connectors. Since the Raspberry Pi 4 features built-in Wireless and Bluetooth, the possibility of requiring more ports is minimal since the required peripherals are a keyboard, mouse, and should you choose to add one, a webcam.

#: 4-pole stereo audio/video jack

The Raspberry Pi 4 has a 4-pole stereo audio and composite video port used to connect headphones or external speakers.

#: 2-Lane MIPI CSI Camera Port

The Mobile Industry Processor Interface (MIPI) Camera Serial Interface gives you the ability to attach an official Raspberry Pi Camera Module to the motherboard directly.

#: 2-Micro HDMI Ports

The Raspberry Pi 4 also has two micro HDMI ports that allow you to connect the Raspberry Pi to Modern Monitors. The ports support both audio and video with 4Kp60 or 4K resolution support. These two Micro HDMI ports have replaced the full-sized HDMI port available in previous generations of the Raspberry Pi.

#: USB-C Power Port 5V/3A

The Pi 4 has a standard USB Power supply used to power the Raspberry Pi. The Raspberry Foundation recommends using the Official power supply for the Raspberry Pi to avoid voltage and power issues that may damage the device.

Like most single board computers, the Raspberry Pi supports 5V or 3 Amperes power input. The Power supply in Raspberry Pi 4 has changed to USB-C from a Micro USB jack available in previous models.

#: 2-Lane MIDI DSI display ports

The MIDI Display Interface port gives you the ability to connect a display directly to the Raspberry Pi 4.

#: Micro SD Slot

Like older Pis, the Raspberry Pi 4 has an SD Card slot that acts as the hard drive for the board.

#: 2.4/5GHzWireless and Bluetooth 5.0

The Raspberry Pi 4 has a dual-band 2.4 and 5.0 GHz IEEE 802.1/* wireless connectivity and a Bluetooth 5.0 and LE. The wireless connectivity update makes the Pi 4 better than older models —in terms of connectivity.

The above are the essential Raspberry Pi 4 features you should be aware of on the hardware side of things. With these features looked at, we can now move on to discussing how to set up your Raspberry Pi 4.

Section 2

Setting Up the Raspberry Pi 4

"A user interface should be so simple that a beginner in an emergency can understand it within 10 seconds.

Ted Nelson

Like most other computers —except a select few models— the Raspberry Pi 4 is easy to set up and use. However, for it to function properly, it relies on external peripheral devices.

In this section, we are going to cover how to set up the Raspberry Pi 4 and have it up and running.

If you acquired the Raspberry Pi 4 starter kit, you have everything required to run your Pi 4 at full capacity. However, if you did not get the starter kit, you will need various devices before you can set up the Raspberry Pi 4. This include:

#: *USB Power Supply*

[4]**Figure 4 Image Credit iStock**

To power the Raspberry Pi 4, you will need a Power supply rated 2.5 amps or 12.5 Watts with a micro USB-C power connector. You should use the recommended and official power supply for the Raspberry Pi 4.

The Raspberry Pi 4 model uses a USB-C power supply rated 3.0 amps. The figure below shows the Raspberry Pi 4 power supply specifications.

Raspberry Pi
AC ADAPTOR
INPUT: 100-240V-50/60/Hz 0.5A
OUTPUT: 5.1V 3.0A

#: *MicroSD Card*

Like any other computer, the Raspberry Pi requires a storage device for the Operating system, installed programs, and other files.

You can use an 8GB microSD to run the Raspberry Pi 4. However, a 16GB or higher is better to allow room for expansion.

The Raspberry Pi 4 starter kit comes with an SD card installed with NOOBS (New Out of the Box Software), which helps you to install the Operating system with ease. We shall discuss how to install NOOBS on a blank SD card.

#: Keyboard and Mouse

5**Figure 5 Image Credit Shutterstock**

You will also need a keyboard and mouse that you can use to control the device and interact with the user interface. You can use any wired or wireless keyboard and mouse. Wireless devices are, however, not ideal as they may interfere with the networking capabilities of the Raspberry Pi.

For functionality purposes, you can purchase a Raspberry Pi Keyboard and hub that provides more room for additional peripherals.

#: HDMI or Micro HDMI cable

You will need an HDMI cable to connect the Raspberry Pi to an external monitor. Newer models of the Pi, like the Raspberry Pi 4, use a micro-HDMI cable, while older models use large HDMI cables. However, if you are using a monitor with no HDMI port, there's no need to spend a lot of money on an HDMI cable.

If you're using a computer monitor that does not have an HDMI socket, you can buy an HDMI-DVI-D DisplayPort or a VGA adapter.

If you intend to connect your Raspberry Pi 4 to an older TV that uses a composite video or a SCART socket, use a 3.5mm tip-ring-sleeve (TRRS) audio/video cable.

#: A network Cable

If you intend to connect the Raspberry Pi to a wired network, you will also require a network cable. Models such as the Raspberry Pi 4 B support wireless connectivity and may not require a network cable. If you are using an older model, you can use an RJ45 cable.

[6]**Figure 6 Image Credit iStock**

The Raspberry Pi is safe to use without a case, provided you don't place it on a metal surface, which could lead to electrical conduction, thereby causing the motherboard to short-circuit.

Although optional, a case can provide additional protection; the Starter Kit includes the Official Raspberry Pi Case.

Setting Up The Raspberry Pi Hardware

Now let us get set up the Raspberry Pi 4 hardware and install the Operating System.

NOTE: Before you get started, ensure that you have acquired all the discussed peripherals.

The Raspberry Pi 4 is a robust, high-quality computer. However, you should still exercise care when handling and using the device. Always hold the Raspberry Pi board by the edges, never by its flat side where the components are.

Additionally, always ensure that all the metal pins on the board and in good condition and not bent as this will make installing additional hardware very difficult or cause a short circuit that damages the device. As discussed previously, you should also be familiar with the components of the Pi, including what each does.

Once you buy a Raspberry Pi 4, the first step to take is to assemble the device case. If you are using the official Raspberry Pi case, start by splitting the case into the upper and lower parts. Red and white.

Hold the red base in a way that ensures the raised end is facing to your left and the lower end to your right.

7**Figure 7 Image Credit Shutterstock**

Take the Raspberry Pi and hold it by its USB and ethernet ports. With the GPIO header facing upward, slide the Raspberry Pi's left side at a 30-degree angle until it's in place and slowly lower the right side of the Raspberry Pi into place.

If you are using an older model of the Raspberry Pi, select the two side covers, then select the one with the cut-outs for the power connector, HDMI, and audio jack, and carefully line it up with these components on the Raspberry Pi. Next, carefully push it into place, ensuring you do not force it or damage the device in any way.

Take the other side piece and place on the GPIO header side and push it until you hear it click into place, as shown in the figure below:

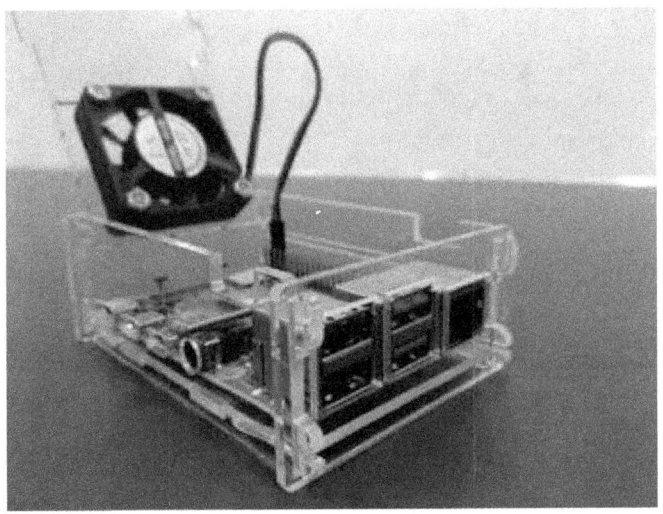

[8]**Figure 8 Image Credit Shutterstock**

Next, for the Raspberry Pi 4 users, simply select the top cover and place it into place to cover the device.

For older models, take the red plastic upper piece and place the two clips at the left into the matching holes on the left of the base, above the microSD card slot. When they're in place, push the right-hand side (above the USB ports) down until you hear a click.

9**Figure 9 Image Credit iStock**

Finally, take the white lid and hold it so that the Raspberry Pi logo is to your right, and the small clips that appear raised on its underside are perfectly aligned with with the hole that's located on the top of the case. Then push it gently downwards until you can hear a click. The click means that your case has been built successfully.

#: Connecting the MicroSD Card

Once you have your Raspberry Pi assembled, we can go ahead and start adding peripherals and storage devices.

First, Select the MicroSD card, which is the main Raspberry Pi storage device. Turn your Raspberry Pi over and slide the MicroSD card into its respective slot. It should slide easily with no pressure.

NOTE: Most SD cards have side guards that help show which direction to place it. The MicroSD should fit into the connector with a click.

To remove the MicroSD card, simply grip its outer end and pull it out gently. Do not forcibly remove the SD card as this may damage the card or the slot. If you are using older models of the Raspberry Pi, you may have to push it inwards and then pull it out gently.

#: Connecting the Mouse and Keyboard

Next, we need to connect the keyboard and mouse so that we can interact with the Pi's user-interface. Select the USB endpoint of the keyboard and place it into one of the USB ports on the Raspberry Pi. Simply do the same for the mouse.

If you are using the official Raspberry Pi keyboard that includes three additional ports to connect to external devices, connect the mouse into one of the Ports on the keyboard and connect the keyboard using the MicroUSB port

[10]**Figure 10 Image Credit Freepik**

Connecting the Mouse and Keyboard should not require any pressure. If anything blocks the ports, do not force the devices. Remove them and examine to ensure that everything is in good condition.

#: Connecting the Display device

The next step is to connect the Raspberry Pi to a display device. Select one end of the HDMI or Micro HDMI —either end is okay— and connect it to the Raspberry Pi.

Select the other end of the HDMI cable and connect it to the display device. If your display has more than one HDMI port, select the port next to the connector and select the Raspberry Pi's port as the display device on your display device.

The Raspberry Pi 4 model comes with two micro HDMI connectors that will need a a good-quality micro HDMI cable. More precisely, this will be necessary when you are connecting to 4K monitors. The figure below shows a Micro HDMI supported by the Raspberry PI 4.

Figure 11 Image Credit iStock

If you are using a TV or monitor that doesn't have an HDMI connector, you can use Adapter cables that allow you to convert the HDMI port on the Raspberry Pi to DVI-D, VGA.

DVI Cables

You can use HDMI to DVI cables to connect your display to the Raspberry Pi. DVI cables do not support audio.

Raspberry Pi4 Made Easy

[11]**Figure 12 Image Credit iStock**

VGA

For VGA monitors, you can use an HDMI to VGA adapter to connect the Raspberry Pi.

[12]Figure 13 Image Credit Freepik

#: *Composite Ports*

The Raspberry Pi contains a composite out port used to connect to analog devices, although the connector type is dependent on the model. The first model of the Raspberry Pi was equipped with an RCA connector, and a standard RCA composite video.

Other models —the Raspberry Pi B+ and later— combine the audio out and composite out on to the same 3.5mm jack plug. That requires a particular type of lead, with audio left on the tip, audio right on ring 1, ground on ring 2, and video on the sleeve. That is the same as leads used on the Zune and Apple devices.

[13]Figure 14 Image Credit Shutterstock

#: Connecting the Raspberry Pi to a Network

You can connect the Raspberry Pi to a wired network —or not. For newer models of the Raspberry Pi that support wireless connections, you will need to install an Operating system to connect to your access point.

For a wired network, select the RJ45 cable —commonly called an Ethernet cable— and plug one end into the Ethernet port on the Raspberry Pi and the other end to a free Ethernet port on your router, hub, or switch.

NOTE: As you do this, ensure that the plastic clip aligns properly to the Ethernet port. You can remove the Ethernet cable by pushing the plastic clip inwards and pulling out gently.

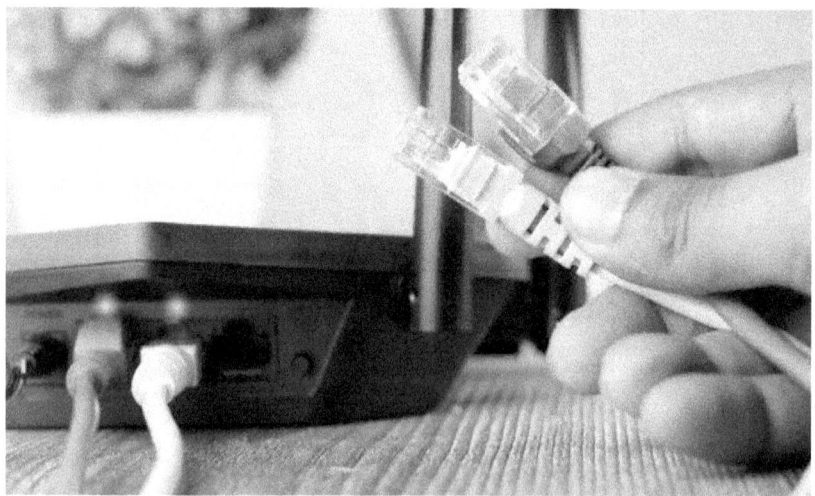

[14]Figure 15 Image Credit Shutterstock

#: Connect the Power Supply

After connecting all the hardware to the Raspberry Pi, the final step is to connect the Power supply. You should only connect the power supply when everything is ready and set up, ready to install the software.

Unlike normal computers, the Raspberry Pi does not have a power switch. It will automatically power on or off once you connect or disconnect it to a power supply.

First, select the end of the Micro-USB power supply and connect it to the Raspberry Pi power port with the narrow part of the micro-USB port facing downward. It should slide gently with minimal pressure.

[15]**Figure 16 Image Credit iStock**

If you purchased the Official Raspberry Pi power supply, you should have various connectors designed to be compatible with different countries. Select the one that suits you and connect to the PSU body until it clicks into place.

Finally, connect the Raspberry Pi Power supply to the main socket and power on the socket. The Raspberry Pi will automatically boot up.

Section 3

Installing Raspberry Pi Software

"The only thing I understand deeply, because in my teens, I was thinking about it, and every year of my life, is software. So I'll never be hands-on on anything except software."

Bill Gates

Before you can begin using the Raspberry Pi 4 to perform computation tasks, you will need to set up the software that will drive the computer: *the Operating system*. We will use the official, easy-to-use, and compatible software designed to perform this task.

Using the New-Out-Of-the-Box (NOOBS) software, we can choose the Operating system to install based on how we intend to use the Raspberry Pi 4. The NOOBS software is so intuitive that its installation requires but a few clicks.

If you have the official Raspberry Pi starter kit, your bundled SD card will come with a pre-installed NOOBS software. As such, you can feel free to skip to the next section of the installation. If not, follow the guide on how to flash the NOOBS software on your MicroSD card.

The NOOBS installer has the Official Raspbian OS, which is the official OS designed for the Raspberry Pi as well as other alternative operating systems downloaded from the internet and installed during the installation process.

Let's get started:

How to Flash NOOBS to SD Card (Project #1)

We can use various approaches to install the NOOBS to the SD card. For the sake of diversity, we will cover dual options.

#: Method 1

The first step is to grab a copy of the NOOBS archive from the official Raspberry site. You can do that by heading to the following resource page:

https://www.raspberrypi.org/downloads/noobs/

The NOOBS software is available in two flavors: The main file that contains the Raspbian OS and installs offline and the Lite version that requires the Raspberry Pi to have an active internet connection so that the proves can download the OS images.

You should download the main version:

Raspberry Pi4 Made Easy

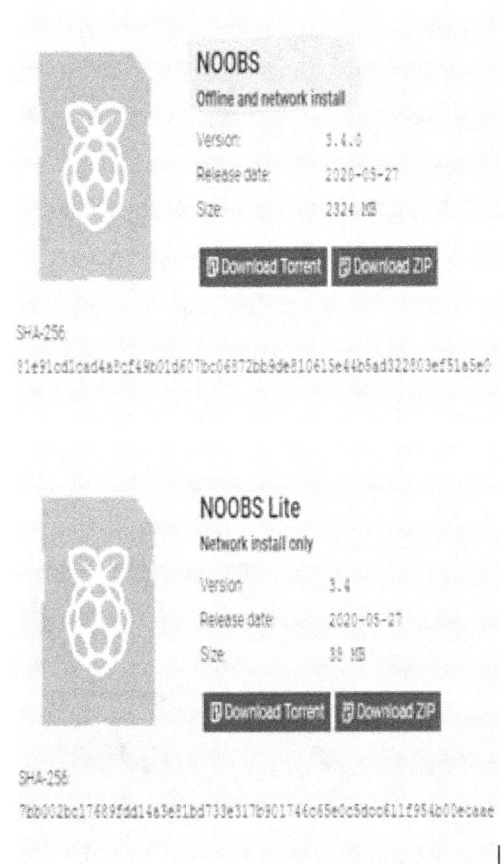

You can download a direct zip archive. Alternatively, if you're a big fan of peer-to-peer, you can download it as a torrent file.

Once you have the file downloaded, we can start installing it on the microSD card. Insert your SD card into a computer —

other than the Pi 4— and download the SD card Formatter available on the resource page below:

https://www.sdcard.org/downloads/formatter/

Once downloaded, install the software and launch it so that you can format the SD card and make it ready to install the software. Make sure you select the correct SD card in the "Select Card" option, select FAT32, and click format. Once completed, we can move to the next step.

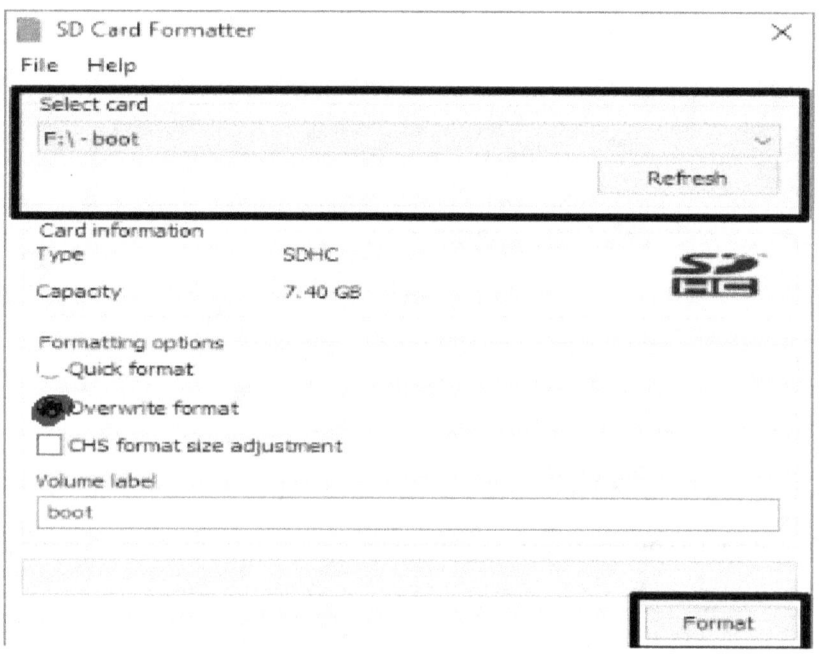

Figure 20: SD Card Formatter options

NOTE: You can use other methods to format the SD card in FAT32 formats such as Gparted in Linux, diskpart in Windows, or Disk Utility in OSx.

Next, open the NOOBS zip archive we download and extract it using your favorite archiver. Once extracted, copy all the files and paste them in the root of the SD card. Ensure you copy the files in the archive, not the archive itself as shown below:

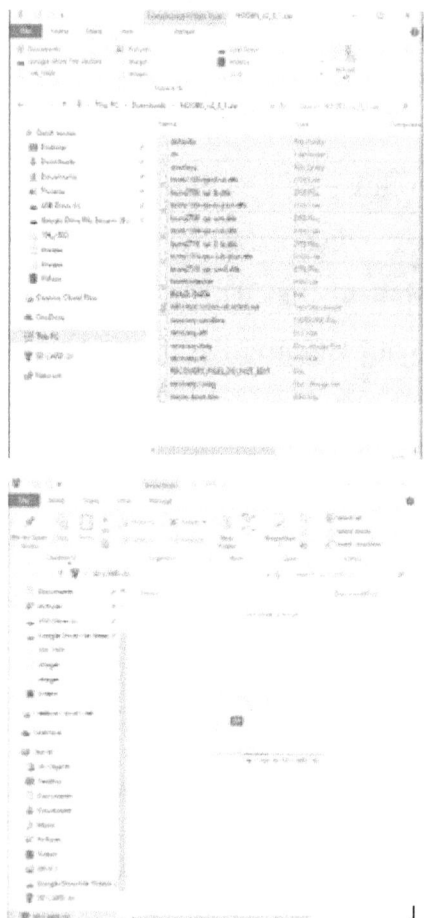

With this done, we have now set up the NOOBS software, and it's ready to install. Before we begin the installation process, let us look at the other method you can use to install NOOBS.

#: Method 2

Open your browser and navigate to the following page:

https://www.raspberrypi.org/downloads/

Once there, download the Raspberry Pi imager for your Operating system and install it.

Launch the application and select "Choose OS," which will open a dialog that will allow you to choose an Operating System (OS) you wish to install —as shown in the figure below:

Raspberry Pi4 Made Easy

You can install a wide range of OS such as Raspbian OS, LibreELEC, Ubuntu server, etc. For the sake of simplicity, select Raspbian OS (other) and choose "Full."

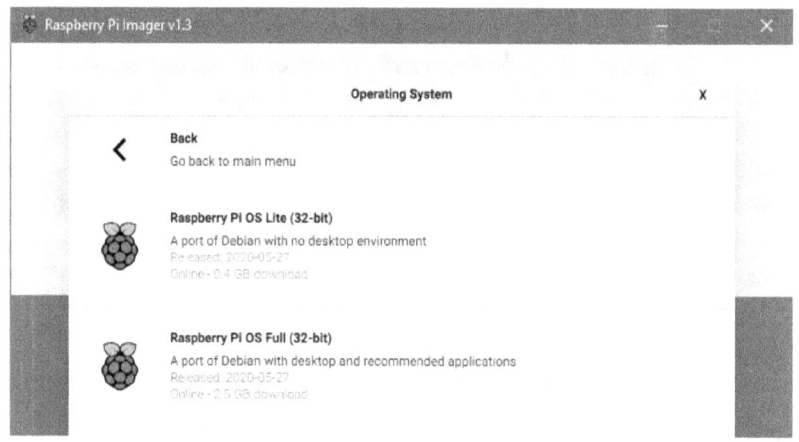

Raspberry Pi4 Made Easy

Next, choose the SD card you wish to write the image to, and finally, click "Write."

If you already have a Raspbian OS archive download or another custom image such as Mozilla WebThings —we will discuss how to set up this in the projects section— Select the custom options and select the image archive.

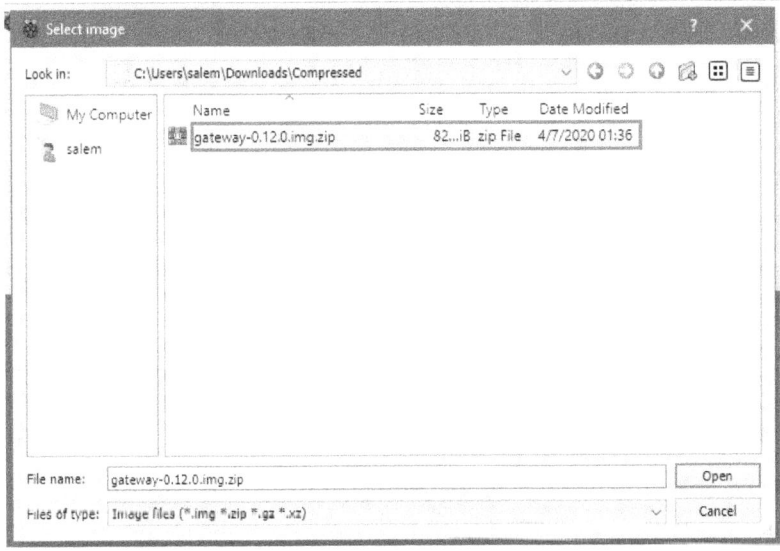

You can also use the Raspberry Formatter to format the SD card. The Formatter also allows you to flash the bootloader for recovery options.

Once completed, you can move to the installation process.

How to Set Up NOOBS on Linux (Project #2)

In this subsection, we are going to cover how to install NOOBS on Linux. We are going to use the Terminal to perform the partitioning and extraction.

While this process may seem detailed and intimidating, you should nevertheless work through it because the knowledge you gain will prove instrumental as you work with the Raspberry Pi to set up innovative projects.

For this guide, we shall use the latest version of Debian. However, any Linux distribution with the correct utilities installed will work fine.

Step 1

Launch the Terminal and enter the command: sudo fdisk -l to list all the connected disks and partitions in the operating system. Ensure to run the command as root or using an account that has elevated privileges.

Step 2

The output will be something close to /dev/sda or /dev/sdb, which indicates disk 1 and disk 2. If you have more than two drives connected, you may get /dev/sd(n) where n is the alphabetical number of the devices connected.

Step 3

Once you locate your SD card in the listed devices, copy its identity code and proceed to the next step.

Step 4

The next step is to repartition and format the SD card using the FAT32 filesystem.

To do that, use the command: sudo fdisk /dev/sda, replacing the /dev/sda with the code representing your SD card.

Step 5

Once you run the above command, you should see command m for help. Press enter to view all the commands available in the fdisk utility.

We are only going to use the command d to delete all the partitions currently made on the SD card and command n to create a new partition.

Step 6

Now enter the command d and press enter. Enter 1 for the partition number. If there are other partitions in the SD card, enter command p to print them, then select enter command d and enter their corresponding partition number. Repeat this procedure until you delete all the partitions on your SD card.

Step 7

Once you're sure you have deleted all the partitions, the next step is to create a new one so that you can install NOOBS.

While still in fdisk, enter the command n and press Enter. Enter the command p to confirm the partition type as Primary and proceed.

Now enter the partition number as 1 and click enter. Next, Enter the First and Last sector or press Enter to confirm the defaults.

Step 8

To confirm that the SD Card contains only one partition, enter the command p to list all the available partitions.

Step 9

To change the Filesystem from Linux to FAT32, enter the command L to list all the codes available. Once you locate the code corresponding to FAT32, enter it and click Enter. In this case, we shall select the t and b commands, respectively.

Once the operation is successful, the Terminal shall display a message indicating that the partition has successfully changed to FAT32.

Step 10

Once you are sure the implementation of the changes is a success, enter the command w to write all the changes to the disk and confirm.

Step 11

Once we have finished creating the partition, we can format it by entering the command sudo mkfs vfat /dev/sda/, where dev/sda represents the code for your SD card. These commands tell Linux to create a filesystem on the FAT32 partition of your SD card.

Step 12

Once the command has executed and successfully formatted the SD card, we need to download NOOBS, extract, and copy all the files into the SD card.

Step 13

You can download NOOBS by navigating to the resource page below. As mentioned earlier, make sure you select the latest Zip or Torrent download of NOOBS and not NOOBS Lite.

https://www.raspberrypi.org/downloads/noobs/

For this book, we shall use the Wget tool to download the file from the Linux terminal. Navigate to the folder you want to download the file to, for this case, the Downloads folder, by entering the command cd ~/Downloads.

Once in the download folder, enter the command

wget -c https://downloads.raspberrypi.org/NOOBS/images/NOOBS-2019-09-30/NOOBS_v3_2_1.zip

Once you execute the command, wait for the download to complete.

Step 14

Once the download process completes, locate where the SD card is mounted by executing the command sudo fdisk -l and find the code. Now enter the command sudo mount | grep -i sdb.

Once mounted, navigate to the SD card by entering the command cd /media/username/<device name>

Step 15

Once in the SD Card root directory, extract the files by executing the command:

unzip ~/Downloads/NOOBS_v3_2_1.zip

This command will automatically extract all the necessary files into the SD card.

NOTE: You can complete the formatting process using other utilities such as gParted. When using formatting utilities, take care not to Format Your System's directory.

How to Install Raspbian OS

With the SD card containing NOOBS connected to the Raspberry Pi, connect the power supply, and boot the device.

Once booted up with a fresh installation of the NOOBS software on the MicroSD card, the interface shall prompt you with a welcome screen, a Raspberry logo, and a progress bar on top of the screen.

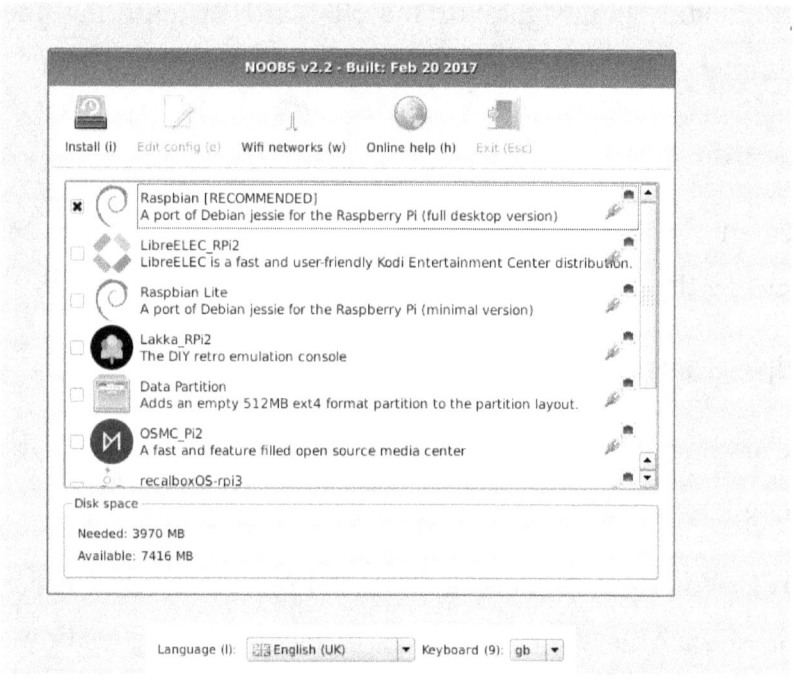

You shall also see a list of optional Operating systems you can install. Some of the Operating systems included in the NOOBS software include:

Raspberry Pi OS	LibreELEC	OSMC
Recalbox	Lakka	RISC OS
Screenly OSE	Windows 10 IoT Core	TLXOS

If you are using NOOBS version 1.3.10 and higher, you can only install Raspbian OS installed offline; installing the other Operating systems will require network access.

At the time of writing this book, the latest version of the NOOBS software is version 3.3.1. Therefore, your interface — as shown in figure 26— may differ depending on available versions.

If your display is not working, ensure that you have the display properly connected and that you are using the correct input media on your display.

Once you have selected the Operating system you wish to install, in this case, Raspbian OS, which is a Debian flavor OS customized for the Raspberry Pi, you can use the mouse to mark the left of "Raspbian Full" option.

Upon selecting the Operating system, the install option will become active, thus allowing you to install the software.

Next, click the install option and select "YES" to confirm the message, thereby accepting the overwriting of all the data on the SD card —this does not include NOOBS software.

Confirming will initialize the installation process, which can take approximately 10 to 20 minutes, depending on the read/write speed of your MicroSD card. You will see a progress bar and some features about the Raspberry Pi. We will get to know Raspbian OS better in later sections.

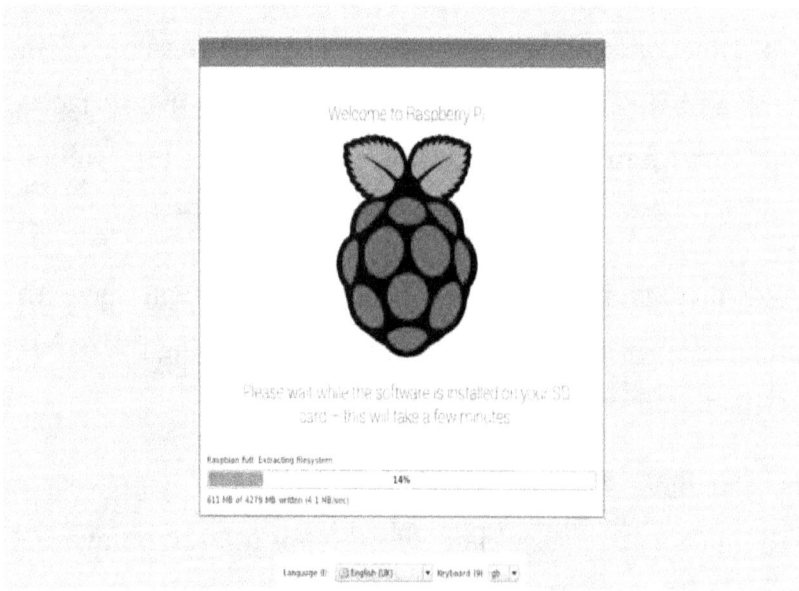

Raspberry Pi4 Made Easy

NOTE: Do not interrupt the installation process, for instance, by ejecting the SD card during the installation or unplugging the power supply.

If you experience any power interruption during installation, unplug the power supply from the PI and hold down the SHIFT key and power on the Raspberry Pi to bring boot into recovery mode. Doing this brings up the Raspbian Menu and allows you to reinstall your operating system.

Once the installation process completes, the Raspberry Pi will reboot and start in the newly installed Operating system. The first boot may take a while as the Pi performs configuration and adjustments to utilize the space on the SD card efficiently.

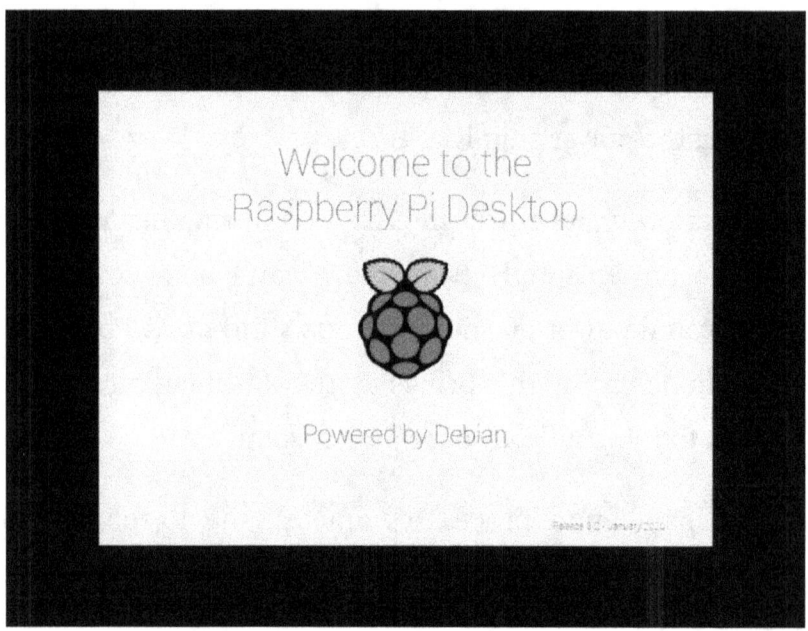

Once the boot process completes, the Pi will launch the Raspbian Desktop and initializes the setup process.

With our Pi 4 set up, we can now move on to the next section where we shall start learning how to work with the Raspbian Pi OS.

Section 4

Working With Raspbian OS

"We've gone through the operating system and looked at everything and asked how can we simplify this and make it more powerful at the same time."

Steve Jobs

The Raspberry Pi, like every other computer, is capable of running a wide range of applications and operating systems. However, the most popular OS for the Raspberry Pi is the Raspbian OS, which we installed in the previous section.

The Raspbian OS is a Debian-based distribution, equipped with the Raspbian Pi Desktop, and customized to suit the Raspberry Pi.

The Raspbian desktop is not that different from other desktop environments from Linux —such as GNOME, KDE, XFCE, etc. Even if you have never used a Linux distribution before, you should be in a position to handle it easily.

If you wish to test the Raspbian OS on a virtual machine, you can download the iso image from the following resource page:

https://www.raspberrypi.org/downloads/raspberry-pi-desktop/

How to Set up the Raspberry Pi 4 Using the Wizard

Running the Raspbian OS for the first time will prompt you with a setup wizard —as shown in the figure below.

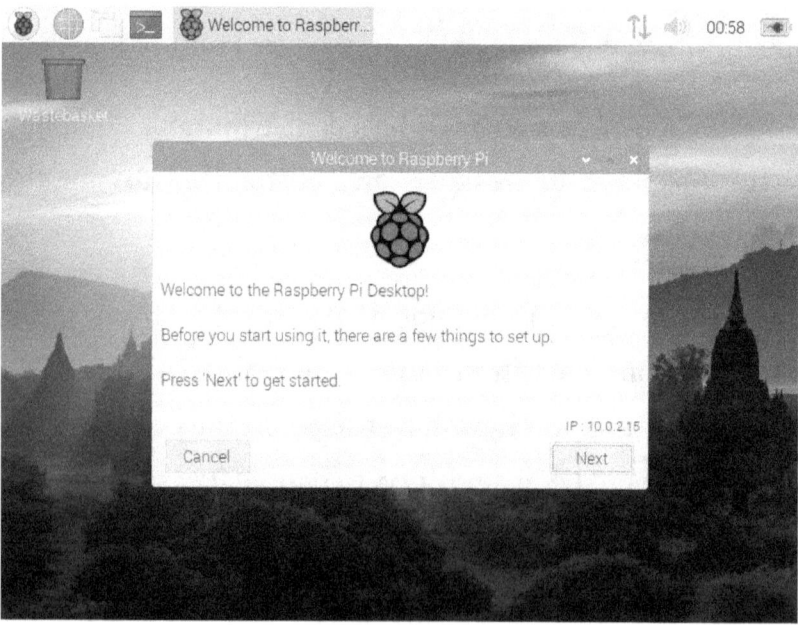

Do not skip this process because some features may not work until after the proper configuration of the Raspberry Pi.

Click "Next" and select your country and language. You should also set the time zone from the list of provided options.

Next, the wizard will prompt you to set a password for the Raspberry Pi. By default, the password is "pi," and the username is "raspberry." Choose a strong password, but one that's also easy to remember, and finally click "Next."

The next screen will prompt you to choose your wireless network. Select the network you wish to connect to and provide the passphrase to connect. If you intend to use a wired connection, you can skip this process.

Wireless connections are available in the latest models of the Raspberry Pi. You can, however, use an external wireless adapter to connect to a wireless network.

The next screen will allow you to choose whether to check and install updates. You can choose to skip this step and do it manually later.

Finally, you will get to the Welcome screen, which will prompt you to reboot your Raspberry Pi to apply the set changes.

Let us go over some of the basics of navigating the Raspbian Desktop. Although this is not mandatory, it will certainly help you work with the Raspbian Desktop more easily, especially if you have never used a Linux distro before.

How to Navigate The Raspbian Desktop (Like a Pro)

Like most Operating systems, the desktop has a wallpaper as a background. At the top of the desktop, you will find a taskbar that shows running applications. The top left side has the Raspberry icon that shows the Menu of installed applications. Next is the web icon, followed by the File Manager and the Terminal.

On the top right corner is the System Tray with icons such as Media Effect, Time, CPU monitor, Sound control, Network connection, and Bluetooth for supported models.

You can use the Menu to search for applications you want to use. By default, the Raspberry Pi comes equipped with the Chromium browser that works efficiently. You can, however, install another browser using the Debian package Manager — we shall cover how to do this in later sections.

Interacting with files with the default file manager is easy. Like all Linux systems, each user has a home directory that allows the said user to store files isolated from other users. You can also interact with the File system from the command prompt.

NOTE: There's a ton we've left unsaid about basic concepts related to working with the Raspbian Desktop. We've overlooked them because most are easy to follow based on previous operating systems and are not essential to becoming a pro-Raspberry Pi user.

Section 5

Installing Software

"I think Linux is a great thing, because Linux is an alternative to Windows, and because, of all the operating systems that are at all relevant today, Unix is the best of a bad lot."

Jamie Zawinski

Although the Raspberry Pi does come with a wide range of pre-installed software, you may need to install software that meets your specific needs.

Since Raspbian is a Debian-based distribution, you can use the apt package manager to install software from the command line.

The Raspbian desktop also features a GUI software installer called "Recommended Software Tool." You can use this tool to search for and install any software you want —as long as it's available. To do so, you will need an active internet connection.

The "Recommended Software Tool" also allows you to uninstall unwanted software with a single click.

Working With The Raspberry Pi 4 Command Line

If you have used a Mac or Windows-based system most of your life, you might be unfamiliar with working with the command line. For Linux users, this may be the only thing you use all day.

A command line or Terminal is a window that sits between the desktop environment and the core part of the Operating System. The command line allows you to control the computer using text commands. Getting familiar with the command line is essential to mastering the Raspberry Pi.

To open the Terminal on the Raspberry Pi, navigate to Menu – terminal.

Linux Terminal Basics

In this subsection, we will go over basic commands that can help you work with the Linux terminal with ease.

NOTE: This book does not go over detailed Linux workflows. It, therefore, is not an 'apt' Linux guide. For more information, consider other books geared towards Linux workflows.

The following commands are common when working with Linux.

- mkdir: Used to create a new directory inside the specified directory

- pwd: Used to get the current working directory

- Sudo: Used to perform the specified Linux command using superuser privileges

- Cp: Used to copy files and directories from one source to the specified destination

- rm: Used to remove the specified files and directories

- help: Used to get help with a specified command

- man: Used to get the manual documentation for the specified tool
- cd: Used to change between directories with the Linux Filesystem

How to Set Up a Static IP (Project #3)

In this subsection, we are going to configure the Raspberry Pi to use a static IP address instead of using a DHCP server.

Step 1

The first step is to check whether DHCP service is running by executing the command sudo service dhcp status

Step 2

If DHCP is not running, execute the following commands consecutively:

sudo systemctl start dhcpd.service

sudo systemctl enable dhcpd

Step 3

Once the commands execute successfully, recheck whether DHCP is running and follow the next command

Step 4

Next, find the DHCP configuration file by executing the command find dhcpcd.conf

Step 5

Once you get the file location of the DHCP configuration file, edit it using the command line text editor Nano. Execute the following command.

sudo nano /etc/dhcpcd.conf

Step 6

If you have connected your Raspberry Pi via a cabled Ethernet, the interface is eth0 and wlan0 for Wi-Fi connections.

Step 7

Enter the following lines in the Raspberry Pi DHCP configuration file.

The interface entry should contain the interface you have connected the Raspberry Pi to; for Ethernet, eth0, and wlan0 for Wireless.

NOTE: Use either eth0 or wlan0, not both

For static IP, set the desired IP address for the Raspberry Pi. The IP should not be one assigned to other devices on the same network. Additionally, the IP should be within the subnet range. For example, 192.168.0.2 to 192.168.0.254

Static routers should have the IP address of the router. By default, this is 192.168.0.1. You can also specify the DNS servers you would like to use. If you do not know, set it to the IP address of the router; otherwise, define it.

Step 8

Save the file and reboot the Raspberry Pi.

Step 9

Once rebooted, test the TCP/IP stack. Open the Terminal and enter the command ping raspberrypi.local

```
$ ping raspberrypi.local
Pinging raspberrypi.local [192.168.137.72] with 32 bytes of data:
Reply from 192.168.137.72: bytes=32 time=1ms TTL=64
Reply from 192.168.137.72: bytes=32 time<1ms TTL=64
Reply from 192.168.137.72: bytes=32 time<1ms TTL=64
Reply from 192.168.137.72: bytes=32 time<1ms TTL=64

Ping statistics for 192.168.137.72:
    Packets: Sent = 4, Received = 4, Lost = 0 (0% loss),
Approximate round trip times in milli-seconds:
    Minimum = 0ms, Maximum = 1ms, Average = 0ms
```

The more you continue working with Terminal command — the internet is your friend here; it'll help you learn other commands not covered in this book— the easier it shall be to master it.

Let's now discuss how to access the Raspberry Pi remotely:

Section 6

Connecting the Raspberry Pi Remotely

"When wireless is perfectly applied, the whole earth will be converted into a huge brain, which, in fact, it is, all things being particles of a real and rhythmic whole. We shall be able to communicate with one another instantly, irrespective of distance."

Nikola Tesla

Virtual Network Computing or VNC is a remote access technique that gives you remote control of one computer from another. The technology can help you communicate with servers and cloud computers from the basic Windows or Mac computer.

Since the Raspberry Pi does not feature a built-in monitor, it is best to control it using a terminal or desktop environment from another computer.

Virtual Network Computing (Project #4)

Here is how you can do that:

Step 1

Setting up VNC may require terminal commands based on the distribution you are setting it in. For Raspberry Pi, the PIXEL desktop makes it very easy.

Step 2

To navigate to the Raspberry Pi VNC configuration, click on Menu −> Preferences −> Raspberry Pi Configuration −> Interfaces and enable VNC

Step 3

Once activated, a new icon marked VNC shall appear on the top-right menu bar. Click the icon to open the VNC server settings.

Here, you will see a section labeled "Ready for Connections" and "Get Started" section. You can view the instructions by clicking on the arrow next to the "Get started section."

Step 4

Note the IP address the Raspberry Pi is using, which you can find under the "Get started" section. You can also use ifconfig to see the Raspberry Pi's IP address.

Step 5

Save the VNC server signature and catchphrase that contains a list of randomly generated words.

Step 6

Download and install a VNC viewer software that will enable you to control the Raspberry Pi remotely. Ensure to install it on the device you wish to manage the Pi from, not the Raspberry Pi.

Visit the web page below to download Real VNC.

https://realvnc.com/download/viewer

Install the software on your device; the software is compatible with any Operating System.

Step 7

Once installed, Launch VNC viewer and provide the IP address of the Raspberry Pi you noted from step 5. Under Encryption, select "Let VNC server choose" and click connect.

Step 8

Provide the username and password for the Raspberry Pi. If you are using default credentials, they are username: pi, password: raspberry.

Step 9

Ensure the catchphrase and the signature are valid to ensure you are connecting to the right device.

Step 10

Once connected, the VNC viewer will display the PIXEL desktop environment as if you were using the Raspberry Pi on an actual, connected monitor.

How to Connect to The Raspberry Pi Remotely Via SSH

Another way to connect to the Raspberry Pi remotely is via SSH. To connect the Raspberry Pi via SSH, open the Terminal or Command prompt on Mac, Linux, or Windows.

On the Raspberry Pi, use ifconfig to note down the IP address. On your computer's Terminal, enter the command ssh pi@192.168.0.8, where the pi is your Raspberry Pi's username, and the 192.168.0.8 is your Raspberry Pi's IP address.

Once connected, enter the password for the pi username to connect. Unless you have configured SSH to run on a different port, the default port should work.

Section 7

Configuring the Raspberry Pi

"UNIX is basically a simple operating system, but you have to be a genius to understand the simplicity."

Dennis Ritchie

How to Set up the Configuration File

Unlike a standard computer, the Raspberry Pi does not have a BIOS feature that you can use to control the boot process. Instead, it has a configuration file stored on the SD card and launched during the boot process, thus acting as the Raspberry Pi's BIOS.

The configuration file also helps flash the Raspberry Pi bootloader if any form of corruption occurs. The ability to control the boot parameters of the Raspberry Pi is useful when working with certain types of projects.

You can find the boot configuration file in /boot/config.txt in Linux distributions. On Windows and Mac, you can access it by navigating the folders of the SD Card.

To edit the configuration file, you need root access; any changes you make to the configuration file take effect after rebooting the Raspberry Pi.

While editing the configuration file, you must follow the correct format because incorrect edits might prevent the Raspberry Pi from booting.

The right format for each entry in the configuration file is property=value. Each entry in the file takes up one line.

Newer models of the Raspberry Pi feature a # before the configuration file, acting as disabled entries, which requires you to 'uncomment' them by removing the # symbol before the entry.

The following are examples of entries in the Raspberry Pi configuration file.

```
# Force the monitor to HDMI mode so that sound will be sent over HDMI cable
hdmi_drive=2
# Set monitor mode to DMT
hdmi_group=2
# Set monitor resolution to 1024x768 XGA 60Hz (HDMI_DMT_XGA_60)
hdmi_mode=16
# Make display smaller to stop text spilling off the screen
overscan_left=20
overscan_right=12
overscan_top=10
overscan_bottom=10
```

You can also view and modify the current settings in the configuration file by using the following commands.

- vcgencmd get_config <config>: We use this command to display a specific configuration value in the file.

- vcgencmd get_config int: We use this command to list all the integer configuration options that are true – meaning non-zero.

- vcgencmd get_config str: We use this command to list all the string configuration options that are true – meaning non-null

You can view most of the configuration settings by using the vcgencmd command. When you use this command, other commands are unavailable.

Configuration Settings

Here, we are going to discuss some configurations edits you can perform to make the Raspberry Pi more functional according to based on your needs.

We shall categorize them into the sections Memory, Camera, Video/Display, Networking, Boot, Overclocking, and Audio.

#: *Memory Configuration Edits*

These are the most useful memory configuration edits for the Raspberry Pi.

For newer models of the Raspberry Pi, uncomment the disabled entries by removing the # sign.

- disable_l2cache: We use this command to disable or enable ARM access to the GPU cache in the Raspberry Pi. We enable it by setting the value to 1; it requires a corresponding L2 disabled kernel. The default value may differ on various models —such as those with standalone L2 cache.

- gpu_mem: Refers to the memory available from the GPU of the Raspberry Pi, including VPU, HVS, and other Legacy Codecs. We use this edit to set the memory split between the ARM and GPU of the Raspberry Pi. By default, the GPU memory is in megabytes. To avoid performance issues, always allocate the lowest possible value to allow the Linux system as much memory allocation as possible.

- gpu_mem_256: This is the GPU memory in Megabytes for the 256MB for the Raspberry Pi. The 512MB

Raspberry Pi usually ignores it, and the configuration overrides the gpu_mem. The max value for this entry is 192; by default, it does not have a set value.

- gpu_mem_512: This configuration sets the GPU memory in megabytes for the 512MB Raspberry Pi. The configuration becomes redundant and ignored if the memory size of the Raspberry Pi is not 512 MB. Likewise, it overrides the gpu_mem entry with a maximum value of 448MB; the default value is unset.

- gpu_mem_1024: We use this to set the GPU memory in Megabytes for the Raspberry Pi devices with 1024MB of memory or more. If the memory of the Raspberry Pi is less than 1024MB, the configuration becomes redundant and thus ignored. The gpu_mem_1024 has a maximum value of 944MB with no default value set.

#: Camera Module Configuration Edits

Below are some of the Raspberry Pi camera module configuration settings. The camera module for the Raspberry Pi appears below:

[16]**Figure 17 Image Credit Shutterstock**

- start_x: We use this to enable the attached camera module in the Raspberry pi.

- gpu_mem: We use this configuration to set the minimum GPU memory for the Camera module.

- disable_camera_led: This configuration setting disables the camera LED from turning on when recording video or taking a picture.

#: *Video/Display Configuration Edits*

Below are the most common video configuration edits relating to video and display options for the Raspberry Pi.

Once again, for the latest model of the Raspberry Pi, uncomment the entries to enable them.

NOTE: Because of the 4K support in Raspberry Pi 4 and 4B, some options may be unavailable in various models.

- sdtv_mode: This configuration defines the TV standard for composite video output. We set each mode by using integral values: 0, 1, 2, 3, 16, and 18, each representing: Normal NTSC, Japanese Version NTSC, Normal PAL, Brazillian PAL, Progressive scan NTSC, and Progressive scan PAL, respectively.

- sdtv_disable_colorbust: This configuration enables or disables color bust on the composite video output. Once you set the value to 1, it disables color outburst; hence, the picture appears sharper in monochrome.

- sdtv_aspect: This configuration defines the aspect ratio for the composite video output. The default integral value 1 represents the ratio 4:3. The integral value 2 represents the aspect ratio of 14:9, and the integral value 3 represents the aspect ratio of 16:9

- enable_tvout: This configuration enables composite output. Only the Raspberry Pi 4 supports this, which by default, disables composite output.

#: HDMI Options

These settings relate to the HDMI settings for the Raspberry Pi. Since Raspberry Pi 4 supports dual HDMI, you can tweak the settings for each HDMI as long as they do not conflict. You can do this by using the entry syntax: <command><hdmi port>

- hdmi_safe: We use this configuration to enable safe mode settings, which tries to boot the Raspberry Pi with the maximum HDMI compatibility configuration. You can also achieve Maximum compatibility configuration by applying the following settings.

```
hdmi_force_hotplug=1
hdmi_ignore_edid=0xa5000080
config_hdmi_boost=4
hdmi_group=2
hdmi_mode=4
disable_overscan=0
overscan_left=24
overscan_right=24
overscan_top=24
overscan_bottom=24
```

Figure 33: Maximum compatibility configuration settings

- hdmi_drive: We use this to choose between HDMI and DVI modes.

- hdmi_ignore_edid: This configuration enables the option to ignore EDID/data for displays that do not have accurate Extended Display Identification Data (EDID).

- hdmi_pixel_encoding: We use this configuration to enforce the pixel encoding mode. By default, EDID requests pixel encoding, and changing the value is not necessary. The integral value 1 represents RGB Limited, 2 for RGB Full, 3 for YCbCr limited (16-235), and 4 for YCbCr full (0-255)

- hdmi_force_hotplug: This mimics HDMI hotplug signal, which makes it appear as if you have an HDMI display attached.

- confi_hdmi_boost: We use this to configure the signal strength for the default HDMI interface.

- display_rotate: We use this configuration to rotate the display clockwise on the enabled monitor. The integral values represent 1 for 90 degrees, 2 for 180, 3 for 270, the hexadecimal code 0x10000 for horizontal flip and 0x20000 for vertical flip.

- hdmi_group: We use this configuration to define the HDMI type.

Hdmi-group	Result
0	Auto-detect from EDID
1	CEA
2	DMT

- framebuffer_width: This configuration helps specify console frame buffer width in pixels, and is similar to frambuffer_height.

- disable_touchscreen: This configuration enables or disables the touchscreen for the target display. The value 1 enables while 0 disables this option.

The Raspberry has very many Video and Display options that we cannot discuss here in their entirety. For more options, check the Raspberry Pi documentation that you can find on the resource page below:

https://raspberrypi.org/documentation/configuration/config-txt/video.md

#: Network Configuration Edits

The Network configuration is not very popular —the Raspberry Pi documentation may not have it.

The following is the most common network configuration edit.

- smsc95xx.macaddr: We use this to configure the smsc95xx driver to use a random mac address on each boot instead of the default mac address.

#: Boot Configuration Edits

Here are the boot configuration edits for the Raspberry Pi.

As usual, for newer models of the Raspberry Pi, such as the Raspberry Pi 4, uncomment the required entries by removing the # sign.

- disable_commandline_tags: We use this configuration to stop the start.elf from filling in ATAGS before kernel launch. The ATAGS is the memory before 0x100

- Kernel: We use this to set an alternative name while loading the kernel. The default name is kernel.img, kernel7.img, kernel7l.img, and is of type string.

- Cmdline: We use this configuration to set the command line parameters that can be used instead of the cmdline text file.

- disable_splash: This command enables or disables a splash screen on boot.

For some models, specific entries may be deprecated and obsolete. To find out more about boot options in the config.txt file, use the link provided below:

https://www.raspberrypi.org/documentation/configuration/config-txt/boot.md

#: Overclocking Configuration Edits

The following are the overclocking settings you can enable on the Raspberry Pi. Overclocking has been available in Raspberry Pi models since 2012 without voiding the warranty. However, you should exercise caution to avoid overloading the processor.

NOTE: Setting any overclocking parameters to values other than those used by raspi-config may set a permanent bit within the SoC, making it possible to detect an overclocked Pi.

- arm_freq: Used to set the frequency of the ARM processor in MHz. The default value varies based on models such as 1000 MHz for Raspberry Pi Zero and Raspberry Pi W, 700 MHz for Raspberry Pi 1, 900 MHz for Raspberry Pi 2, 1200 MHz for Raspberry Pi 3, 1400 MHz for Raspberry Pi 3A+/3B+, and 1500 MHz for the Raspberry Pi 4.

- gpu_freq: Used to set: core_freq, h264_freq, isp_freq, and v3d_freq altogether. The default value for this entry may also vary based on the specified model. For default values, check out the documentation on Overclocking available on the page below:

https://raspberrypi.org/documentation/configuration/config-txt/overclocking.md

- core_freq: Used to set the frequency of the GPU core processor in MHz. On certain models, especially those that came before Raspberry Pi 2, changing to this entry has a parallel impact on the ARM performance.

- h264_freq: Used to set the frequency of the hardware video block in MHz. It acts as an individual override on the gpu_freq entry.

- isp_freq: Used to set the frequency of the image sensor pipeline block.

- v3d_freq: Used to set the frequency of the 3D block in MHz.

- avoid_pwm_pll: It means not to dedicate a pll to PWM audio. It may have a slight effect on analog audio.

- sdram_freq: Used to set the frequency of the Synchronous dynamic random-access memory in MHz.

- force_turbo: Used to enable or disable dynamic cpufreq driver and minimum settings.

- over_voltage: Used to adjust ARM/GPU voltage. The default value is 0, which equates to 1.2v.

- Temp_limit: Acts as overheating protection by setting the clocks and voltages to default when the SoC reaches the set value.

- over_voltage_min: Used to set the minimum value of over_voltage used for dynamic clocking.

- sdram_freq_min: Used to set the minimum value for sdram_freq used for dynamic clocking.

- initial_turbo: Enables turbo mode from boot from a given value in seconds (up to 60 seconds) or until cpufreq sets the frequency. To get more information on the initial turbo, check the resource below:

https://www.raspberrypi.org/forums/viewtopic.php?f=29&t=6201&start=425#p180099

#: Audio Configuration Edits

Here are the configuration edits used by the onboard audio output. These configurations mainly control how analog audio and firmware features enable or disabled on the Raspberry Pi.

- disable_audio_dither: Used to disable dither application.
- enable_audio_dither: Used to enable the dither audio application.
- pwm_sample_bits: Used to adjust the bit depth of the onboard analog audio output.

You can find the documentation on audio configuration from the resource page below:

https://www.raspberrypi.org/documentation/configuration/config-txt/audio.md

NOTE: Other references for the Raspberry Pi configuration are available on the official Wiki:

https://elinux.org/RPiconfig

Section 8

Raspberry Pi 4 Projects

"Try not. Do, or do not. There is no try."

Yoda, The Empire Strikes Back

After covering various aspects of the Raspberry Pi, we have learned enough that we can start experimenting with cool and fun projects —besides the ones we've already covered.

Throughout this part, we will cover some simple and innovative projects that'll help you master and enjoy the Raspberry Pi.

For some projects, you will require additional hardware and coding experience. Although the book will provide the code and explain what it does, it's better to understand it yourself so that you can be able to improve and maintain it.

Some of the projects we shall cover in this section include:

- A Web-server running NGINX

- Nagios system monitor

- A Wi-Fi extender using the Raspberry Pi

- Using Mozilla WebThings

- Raspberry Pi Proxy Server

- Math and Data Computation –Mathematica on Raspberry Pi

- Radio Station With Raspberry Pi

- Building Raspberry Pi for Penetration Testing

- Raspberry Pi Media Center with KODI

- Raspberry Pi Torrenting with Deluge

Before we get started, for projects that require coding, you will have to set up a programming environment. Mainly we will work in Python, but for future projects, we will also discuss how to install the C++ programming environment.

NOTE: This is not a programming guide. As such, the book does not dive deep into how to write programs in the specified computer languages.

How to Install Python 3 On the Raspberry Pi 4 (Project #5)

Raspbian OS comes pre-installed with the latest, stable version of Python, which makes the Pi a swell Python programming platform that you can use to script or work with for data science. Beginners also get a lot from the Raspberry Pi programming default setups since Python is an excellent programming language.

You can launch the Python IDLE shell by selecting Menu –> Programming –> Python IDLE. The Python on the Pi is the default Python package that does not contain additional libraries and packages.

For some reason, if you do not have the Python shell, you can download the Python installation package from the Python resource page below and select your desired version:

https://python.org/downloads

To test whether you have installed Python correctly, open the Terminal and enter the command: Python –version to get the version of Python installed.

C++ Installation (Project #6)

C++ is one of the most powerful programming languages used to create a wide range of applications. Programmers use it to develop games, browsers, embedded systems, and Operating Systems.

This subsection looks at how you can start using C++ on Raspbian OS. To check whether your Raspbian OS has the C++ compiler installed, open the Terminal and enter the command whatis gcc.

If you do not have the compiler pre-installed, you can install it by executing the command sudo apt-get update && sudo apt-get install gcc

You can edit the code in Nano or use the Geany editor pre-packaged in Raspbian. Navigate to Menu –> Programming –> Geany and edit the code.

Once you have that completed, we can get started with the projects.

NGINX Webserver (Project #7)

NGINX Is a web server and a reverse proxy. It is similar to Apache, with a few key differences that we will not cover in this section.

Of the benefits of using NGINX instead of Apache is its capability to work efficiently with very minimal CPU and Memory usage.

To learn more about NGINX, read its official documentation available from the resource below:

https://nginx.org/en/docs/

Requirements:

To set up this project, you will require the following tools and software:

A properly configured Raspberry Pi 2, 3 or 4 —SD card, power supply, and a Running Operating system.

Internet connectivity —Wired Ethernet or Wireless for supported models

Procedure

Before we begin the installation and configuration of NGINX, let us make sure that the Raspberry Pi is up to date using the apt package manager. Run the commands:

sudo apt-get update && sudo apt-get upgrade -y

If you have a web-server or service running on port 80, we highly recommend turning it off or using another free port. If you have Apache, you can uninstall it using the command:

sudo apt remove apache2 && sudo apt autoremove

Once all the updates complete and no other applications are using the port 80, we can start installing NGINX server on the Raspberry Pi.

Enter the commands below to install nginx.

sudo apt-get install nginx -y

With the installation completed, we can start the nginx service using systemctl and configure it. Use the command sudo systemctl start nginx to start nginx.

Once the service is up and running, we can navigate to the website using our local machine IP address using the command hostname -i

Once you have grabbed the IP address of the machine, open it using your web browser, which should display the NGINX welcome page.

With the web-server now running, you can start building websites on your local machine.

Raspberry Pi Wi-Fi Extender (Project #8)

The next project is going to be a simple Wi-Fi extender using the Raspberry Pi 4. We shall not detailedly discuss what a Wi-Fi extender does. All we shall say is that it helps increase the range of a wireless network. A Wi-Fi extender is not completely the same as an access point.

Requirements

A Raspberry Pi

Two Wi-Fi adapters. If your Raspberry Pi has an in-built adapter, as is the case with the Pi 4, you only need one.

Procedure

For this project, we are going to use both DHCP and DNS protocols, which are provided by the dnsmasq package

NOTE: The official documentation is available:

http://www.thekelleys.org.uk/dnsmasq/doc.html

The hostapd daemon.

https://manpages.debian.org/testing/hostapd/hostapd.8.en.html

As usual, we will start by updating our packages using the commands:

sudo apt-get update && sudo apt-get upgrade -y

Next, we need to install the required packages and their dependencies using the commands:

Sudo apt-get install hostapd && sudo apt-get install dnsmasq -y

Next, we need to set up the wireless connection or wlano that we are going to use. If you already have an active connection to a wireless network, you can skip this process.

Next, we need to set up the DHCP server to assign an IP address to the Raspberry Pi. Read section 5 to remind yourself how to configure static IP addresses.

With the Wi-Fi configuration set up, we can modify the hostapd configuration by running the command:

```
sudo vi /etc//hostapd/hostapd.conf
```

Feel free to use any text editor of choice such as Nano for simplicity. In the file, add the following lines to allows us to interact with the wireless device.

```
interface=wlan1
hw_mode=g
channel=6
ieee80211n=1
wmm_enabled=1
ht_capab=[HT40][SHORT-GI-20][DSSS_CCK-40]
macaddr_acl=0
ignore_broadcast_ssid=0
auth_algs=1
wpa=2
wpa_key_mgmt=WPA-PSK
rsn_pairwise=CCMP
ssid=Pi3-WIFIExtended
wpa_passphrase=wifiPassword
```

Change the interface to suit the name of the wireless card assigned by the Operating System. You may need to specify the specific driver the wireless device is using.

Next, we need to edit the hostapd files in /etc/default and /etc/init.d/ because the hostapd daemon uses them to load the configurations.

Enter the command:

sudo vi /etc/default/hostapd

Locate the line #DAEMON_CONF="" and replace it with the line DAEMON_CONF="/etc/hostapd/hostapd.conf"

Next, edit the configuration under the init.d directory using the command:

sudo vi /etc/init.d/hostapd

Similar to the above configuration, locate the single line above and replace it as the same as above.

Now with the hostapd setup, we can configure dnsmasq by editing the configuration.

We start by backing up the old configuration using the command:

sudo mv /etc/dnsmasq.conf /etc/dnsmasq.conf.bak

Once the default configuration backs up, we can start by creating a new configuration file and add new settings with the command:

Sudo vi /etc/dnsmasq.conf

Once the file opens, add the following lines to allow dnsmasq to handle all incoming connections.

interface=wlan1

listen-address=192.168.0.120

bind-interfaces

server=1.1.1.1

domain-needed

bogus-priv

dhcp-range=192.168.0.2,192.168.0.254,24h

Next, we need to edit the system configuration to allow the Raspberry pi to forward all traffic from the first interface to the second interface.

sudo vi /etc/sysctl.conf

Locate the following line and uncomment it by removing the # sign in the beginning.

#net.ipv4.ip_forward=1

Next, we need to edit the configuration tables and add a few rules. Enter the commands below:

sudo iptables -t nat -A POSTROUTING -o wlan0 -j MASQUERADE

sudo iptables -A FORWARD -i wlan0 -o wlan1 -m state --state RELATED,ESTABLISHED -j ACCEPT

sudo iptables -A FORWARD -i wlan1 -o wlan0 -j ACCEPT

Replacing wlan* with the name of your interfaces.

Finally, save the configuration files and load them to ensure the system does not clear them upon reboot. Save all the files and reboot the Pi.

Nagios System Monitor (Project #9)

This project shows you how to set up a Nagios software on your Raspberry Pi.

Nagios is an open-source software used to monitor networks, systems, and other infrastructure. You can learn more about it from the resource page below:

https://www.nagios.org/

Nagios is very lightweight; it allows you to monitor systems and networks using a web interface. Although there are various versions of Nagios, including paid ones, we will use the free version in this guide.

NOTE: This project can help you manage various administration tasks.

Requirements

All you need for this project is a fully functional Raspberry Pi and Internet connection.

Procedure

We are going to build the Nagios core from the source.

We start by ensuring our system is up to date using the command:

sudo apt-get update && sudo apt-get upgrade -y

The next step is to install the required packages to run Nagios. Use the command shown below:

sudo apt-get install -y autoconf gcc libc6 make wget unzip apache2 apache2-utils php libgd2-dev

Download the source code from the GitHub release using wget or normal download: For wget, use the commands:

wget

https://github.com/NagiosEnterprises/nagioscore/releases/download/nagios-4.4.6/nagios-4.4.6.tar.gz

Next, extract the archive with the command:

tar xvf nagios-4.4.6.tar.gz

Next, navigate into the directory so that you can compile and install Nagios.

Once in the directory, enter the commands below to start the compilation process.

./configure --with-httpd-conf=/etc/apache2/sites-enabled

sudo make all

This command will compile and create users that Nagios requires to run properly. Next, we need to add the user www-data to the nagios group created from the above commands.

Next, we need to install the compiled binaries to the operating system using the command make install:

sudo make install

To install and enable the Nagios service at startup, enter the command below:

Sudo make install-deamoninit

To set up an external command directory, enter the commands:

sudo make install-commandmode

Next step, copy the configuration file with the command:

Sudo make install-config

NOTE: The configuration files are vital and Nagios will fail to load if they are corrupt or missing.

We then need to install the Apache configuration files with the command. The configuration files will install to the directory specified using the make command.

To ensure the Apache modules are enabled, we use the a2enmod commands as:

sudo make install-webconf

sudo a2enmod rewrite

sudo a2enmod cgi

Finally, we need to create an apache user that will access the Nagios web interface on the Raspberry Pi.

sudo htpasswd -c /usr/local/nagios/etc/htpasswd.users nagiosadmin

We can then start Apache and Nagios service on the Raspberry Pi using the commands:

sudo /etc/init.d/apache2 restart

sudo systemctl enable nagios

sudo systemctl start nagios

This command will start the Nagios service and configure to enable on bootup.

You can expand the functionality of the Nagios Software by installing plugins.

In the Nagios directory created earlier, download plugins code using wget as shown:

wget https://nagios-plugins.org/download/nagios-plugins-2.3.3.tar.gz

Extract the archive using the command:

tar xvf nagios-plugins-2.3.3.tar.gz

Next, navigate to the nagios plugins directory and start to compile the plugins using the command:

sudo./configure

Once completed, we can begin compiling the plugins using the make command:

This process can take a while, depending on the performance capabilities of the Raspberry Pi. Once completed, install the Nagios plugins using the make install command.

Finally, restart the Nagios daemon to load all the installed plugins using systemctl restart nagios or use the init.d symbolic links.

With everything properly configured and the web interface working, we can access Nagios using the Raspberry Pi's IP address/nagios as:

http://192.168.0.250/nagios

That should connect and bring up the Nagios core welcome page.

Check out the official Nagios documentation to learn more about how to use and configure Nagios to fit your needs.

Mozilla WebThings (Project #10)

The Mozilla WebThings gateway is a software distribution developed by Mozilla for smart home gateways. It allows users to control and monitor their smart home devices over a web interface.

This project will allow us to set up the Raspberry Pi as a smart home device monitor.

Requirements

For this project, you will require the following items:

A Raspberry Pi Board

A MicroSD Card

USB Dongles

All Other necessary peripherals.

Check the following link to see compatible USB dongles.

https://github.com/mozilla-iot/wiki/wiki/Supported-Hardware#usb-dongles

Procedure

The first step for the project is to download Mozilla WebThings gateway image available here:

https://iot.mozilla.org/gateway/

The next step is to flash the image onto our SD card to install it on our device. You can use Raspberry Pi imager —as discussed in earlier sections. For diversity, let's look at how to Flash the Image using balenaEtcher

Download the software for your Operating System from the resource page below and install it:

https://www.balena.io/etcher/

Launch it and select the image which we downloaded from the above section. Ensure that the SD card is inserted and selected in the device section and click Flash.

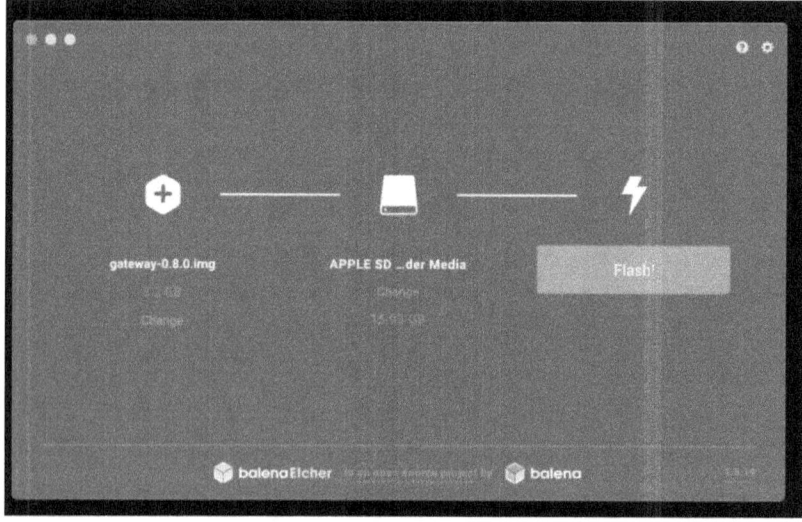

Once the Flash process completes successfully, eject the SD card and insert it into the Raspberry Pi —as discussed in an earlier section.

The next step is to boot the Raspberry Pi, ensuring you have all your peripherals and dongles connected, and wait for the software to boot up.

The initial bootup process may take a while compared to other subsequent bootups.

Once the device has booted up, connect it to your wireless network to start communicating with the Smart devices on your network.

Once all connected, open the browser and navigate to

http://gateway.local

Navigating here should allow you to register a subdomain that allows you to connect to the gateway over the internet using SSH tunneling provided by Mozilla.

Provide a domain name and an email address, and click create. Wait a few moments as the subdomain initializes. Once completed, you can access the web gateway on any device using the subdomain you created. If you wish to connect to the gateway on a local network, skip this process.

The next step allows you to create an account that secures the gateway to the management interface. Once completed, the process will redirect to the "Things" page where you can add devices, manage, and monitor them.

For more information on how to work with Mozilla WebThings, check out the official documentation available here:

https://iot.mozilla.org/docs/gateway-user-guide.html

Raspberry Pi Proxy Server (Project #11)

In this project, we are going to set up our Raspberry Pi to work as a Proxy server using Privoxy.

Privoxy is a non-caching web proxy that modifies web data and HTTP headers. Privoxy is open-source and flexible enough to support both standalone and multi-user networks.

https://www.privoxy.org/

Requirements

All you need for this project is a fully equipped Raspberry Pi connected to the internet.

Procedure

As usual, we start by ensuring that the Raspberry Pi is up to date using the apt command:

sudo apt-get update && sudo apt-get upgrade -y

Next, we need to install Privoxy with the command:

sudo apt-get install privoxy -y

With the package installed, we need to edit the configuration file to ensure that outside networks can access it.

Open the configuration with Nano, vim, or another text editor under /etc/Privoxy/config:

sudo nano /etc/privoxy/config

By default, the Privoxy configuration only listens on the local machine address under 127.0.0.1 on port 8118. Find this configuration setting and remove the loopback address and leave the port as shown:

listen-address 127.0.0.1:8118

listen-address [::1]:8118

and replace it with:

listen-address :8118

Next, save the file and restart the Privoxy service with systemctl using the command:

sudo systemctl restart privoxy

NOTE: Make sure you set the Raspberry Pi network with a static IP address —as discussed in earlier sections.

Next, we need to enable the proxy server on the browser.

For Firefox, navigate to "Preferences" – "Setting" – "Network Settings."

For Chrome users, open "Settings" – "Advanced" – "Open Proxy Settings."

Once you are under proxy settings for your favorite browser, Enter the IP address of the Raspberry Pi you set in the Static IP section of the book. Next, set the Proxy port as 8118 as configured in the Privoxy configuration.

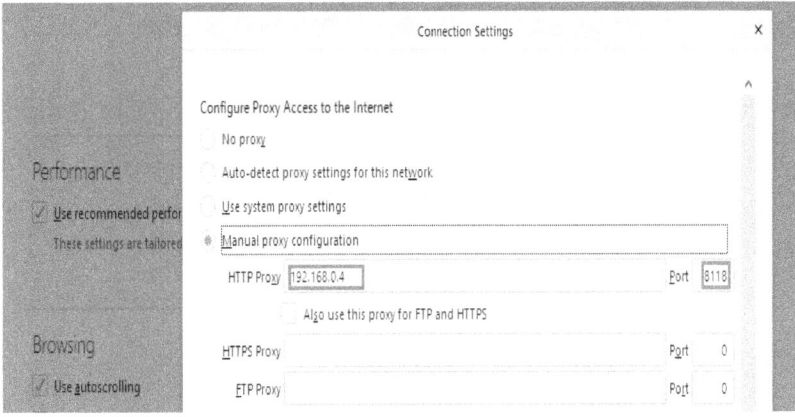

Once you have the proxy settings configured correctly, open your browser and navigate to the following URL:

http://config.privoxy.org

That should provide a Welcome page indicating that the Proxy server is active. If you get an error, ensure the configuration file is correct, and that the Privoxy service is running.

The Raspberry Pi should now be running as a proxy server for all the devices in your network.

Raspberry Mathematica (Project #12)

In this project, we are going to set up a mathematics and data computation engine provided by Wolfram Mathematica.

Mathematic is a powerful data processing engine that is, although available in a paid version, is freely available on Raspberry devices running Raspbian.

For people dealing with data and Wolfram language, you will benefit from this project.

Requirements

Fully Equipped Raspberry Pi

At least 4GB of free space on the SD card

Internet connection

Procedure

NOTE: You should only be running the Raspbian Full Version with a Desktop and all packages installed. Avoid using the Lite version of Raspbian.

As usual, we start by updating the Raspberry Pi with the command:

sudo apt-get update && sudo apt-get upgrade -y

Next, we can install Mathematica from the official Raspbian repositories using the command:

sudo apt-get install wolfram-engine

NOTE: Wolfram engine is a large package; it may take time to download depending on your connection speed. Once the installation process completes, we can launch Mathematica from the Applications menu under Programming.

Doing that will start Mathematica, and you can start to perform mathematical calculations and programs using the Wolfram Mathematica Language.

You can test whether the Wolfram Engine is working as expected. In the available cell, enter 2 + 2, which should display the output. If the output is not 4, it's not working correctly.

In(1)=2+2 + (Enter Button) ←———— Input

Out(1)=4 ←———— Output

If you are new to Mathematica, you can use the following resources to get started and have fun with Mathematics. It will be fun, I promise.

https://www.wolfram.com/language/fast-introduction-for-programmers/en/

https://www.wolfram.com/language/fast-introduction-for-math-students/en/

https://reference.wolfram.com/language/

Raspberry Pi Radio Station (Project #13)

In this cool project, we will set up a radio station using a Radio Transmission Software and the GPIO headers on the Raspberry Pi.

Although the range of the Radio station will not be strong, you can use it to geek out your friends and learn. However, before we go deep into the project, let us discuss how the GPIO headers on the Raspberry Pi work.

In previous sections of the book, we mentioned the GPIO header on the Raspberry Pi. Although we did not discuss it deeply, it is an essential Raspberry Pi feature.

Raspberry Pi4 Made Easy

The GPIO (General Purpose Input/Output) header located alongside the board is on all current models of the Raspberry Pi. The GPIO pins are programmable, and you can set them as output or input to suit the needs for a certain use.

In this section, we will discuss how it works and how to use it for the radio station project.

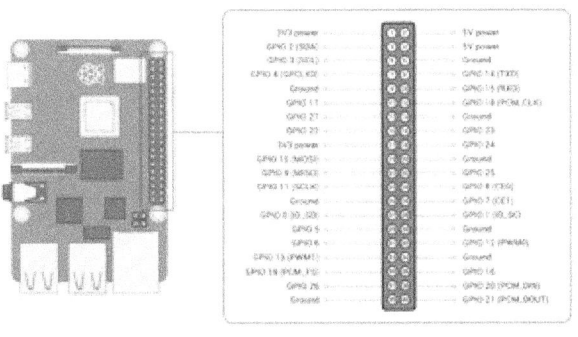

[17]**Figure 18 Image Credit Shutterstock**

The GPIO header on the Raspberry Pi has 20 pins. Some of the pins are available for use with physical devices; others provide power, while others act as communicators with hardware add-ons.

The Pin types fall into various categories classifications, with each category performing specific functions.

Category	Description	Function
3V3	3.3 Volts Power	Permanently-on power source for 3.3volts power
5V	5 Volts Power	Permanently-on power source for 5Volts
Ground	0 Volts Ground	A ground connection mainly used to complete a circuit connected to a power source
GPIO XX	General Purpose Input-Output pin number	Represents GPIO pins available for use by projects — numbered from 2 to

		27
ID EEPROM	Reserved Special-Function pins	PINS reserved for hardware Attached on Top (HAT) etc

Table 2: GPIO header classifications/functions

NOTE: Always connect the Pins carefully to avoid bending them. Do not connect two pins directly to each other, which may short circuit and damage the Pins.

The GPIO is not the only thing you use to work on physical devices. You can use components such as a solderless breadboard that lets you connect components through metal racks hidden beneath its surface instead of connecting them with a bunch of wires. Although not required, this can certainly help.

[18]Figure 19 Image Credit Shutterstock

You can purchase a Canakit Raspberry Pi GPIO breakout board.

The other peripheral you will require are jumper leads, also called jumper connectors. If you are not using a breadboard, jumper connectors will help you connect components to the GPIO header pins. Jumper cables are available in three main versions.

- Male-to-Female: Used to connect the breadboard to GPIO header pins

- Female-to-Female: Used to connect individual components

- Male-to-Male: Used to connect one part of a breadboard to another

If you are working on some complex projects – not covered in this book— you may require all three types of jumper cables.

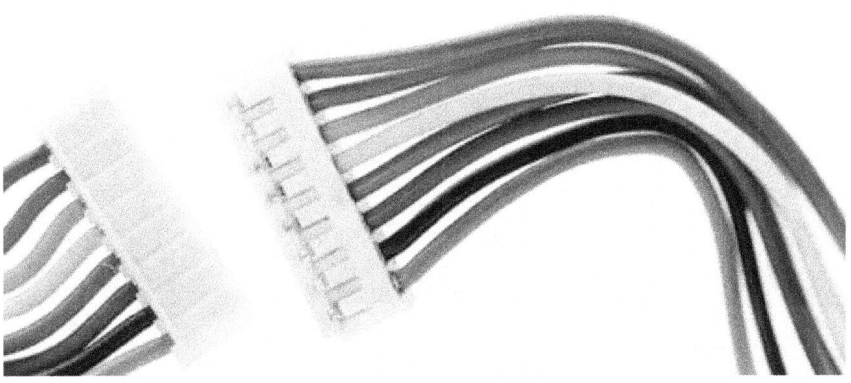

[19]**Figure 20 Image Credit Shutterstock**

Other components you may need include:

- Resistors,

- Light-Emitting-Diode,

- Switch,

- Piezo electronic buzzer, etc.

Check the following resources for more information

https://www.cl.cam.ac.uk/projects/raspberrypi/tutorials/robot/components/resistor/

https://www.electronics-tutorials.ws/resistor/res_2.html

https://www.americanpiezo.com/standard-products/buzzers.html

https://thepihut.com/blogs/raspberry-pi-tutorials/27968772-turning-on-an-led-with-your-raspberry-pis-gpio-pins

Now that we have discussed the basics of the GPIO header and other components of the Raspberry Pi, we can get started with the project.

Requirements

A fully equipped Raspberry Pi

Internet connection

30cm Jumper connector

Procedure

The first step is to connect the jumper connector to the GPIO 4 pin in the header, which will act as an antenna for connecting to the Radio.

Since this project is for educational and fun purposes, you can stick with the default jumper connectors from Canakit.

The next step is to update the packages for the Raspberry Pi and install the Radio software using the command:

sudo apt-get update && sudo apt-get upgrade -y

Once we have updated the packages, we can start to install all the packages we require to create the Radio. The software we are going to use is a C language-written program, and we will have to compile it.

First, we install the required dependencies using the command:

```
sudo apt-get install -y sox make gcc g++ git arecord
libmp3lame-dev -y
```

Once you have all the required packages installed and updated, we can start to install the software. Using git, clone the FM Transmitter Repository from the following resource:

https://github.com/markondej/fm_transmitter

Next, navigate to the cloned directory and remove the .git directory as we will not be contributing to the program

cd fm_transmitter && rm -rf .git

Next, compile the program using the make command.

NOTE: Ensure you are in the fm_transmitter directory when executing this command.

Once the program has compiled on our device, we can test by playing an audio file. You should use a .wav file. The project already includes a test file. Use the command below to start transmitting:

sudo./fm_transmitter -f 100.8 acoustic_guitar_duet.wav

The above command executes the program and transmits the broadcast using a frequency of 100.8. The program supports .wav files, but you can convert other file formats to .wav using the sox command as:

sox my-audio.mp3 -r 22050 -c 1 -b 16 -t wav my-converted-audio.wav

You can add more functionality such as microphone supports using the arecord package as:

arecord -D hw:1,0 -c1 -d 0 -r 22050 -f S16_LE | sudo ./fm_transmitter -f 100.8 –

View the official documentation to learn how to customize the program even better.

Setting Up Raspberry Pi for Penetration Testing (Project #14)

In this project, we are going to set up the Raspberry Pi with a Penetration Testing distribution and make it ready for hacking. This simple project does not require many components

Requirements

Raspberry Pi – Fully Equipped

An SD card – We will have to format it.

Internet connection for the Raspberry Pi

Procedure.

The first step for this project is to download an ISO image for arm devices. We are going to use Kali Linux, which is a very popular and effective penetration testing distributions.

Open the browser and navigate to the resource page below and download the image for your Raspberry Pi model:

https://www.offensive-security.com/kali-linux-arm-images/:

RASPBERRYPI FOUNDATION

Image Name	Torrent	Version	Size	SHA256Sum
Kali Linux RaspberryPi 2, 3 and 4	Torrent	2020.2b	2.1G	ed74ac61c23122daa4776lec43d72d51332acb93ffaa19cf896ae9032efc1c49
Kali Linux RaspberryPi Zero/Zero W	Torrent	2020.2a	2.0G	c760d29e054744352b489e5b616895 4addbb0b597aac67cdeab24f9c06f0a7c0
Kali Linux RPi	Torrent	2020.2a	2.0G	eec60a0f3827c6b004f28fbb9e49f124f495a154f778a1853 6e1a619e1e08f78
Kali Linux RaspberryPi 2 (v1.2), 3 and 4 (64-Bit)	Torrent	2020.2b	2.1G	19061cbdc55a012309c09d4bb8f8dcc9c2ee2f740a5236e7585829e5d8247dd8

The next step is to flash the image on to our SD card. This process will format the previous installation and any Operating system and data saved. Start by opening balenaEtcher and then select an image from the first option.

The latest version of Balena allows you to choose from URL and local files within your local system. Since we have downloaded the image, select the option "Flash from File."

Next, select the target device, which is the SD card for the Raspberry Pi. If you have multiple devices connected, ensure you select the correct device to avoid accidentally wiping the entire device.

Finally, click "Flash" to start writing the image to the SD card. Wait until the process completes, and then move to the next step.

Insert the SD card into the Raspberry Pi and connect the power supply to boot the device. Booting up will launch the Kali Desktop environment that allows you to work in a GUI environment other than SSH.

Login into the desktop using the username "root" and password "toor." Once logged in, you will get the Kali Desktop with all the icons and applications installed.

Now you can start to do all the penetration testing tasks on your Raspberry Pi.

Raspberry KODI Media Center (Project #15)

In this project, we are going to set up a media server for the Raspberry Pi with KODI and OSMC.

OSMC is an open-source media player based on Linux, allowing you to play media from a local network, NAS, and External Networks.

OSMC gets frequent updates, comes packaged as a single Operating System, and because of customization, it can work with the Raspberry Pi with no problems.

You can read more about the OSMC project from the resource page:

https://osmc.tv/

Requirements

A fully equipped Raspberry Pi

Internet connection

Media Source – External Storage or Network Attached Storage

This resource has more information about network-attached storage

https://en.wikipedia.org/wiki/Network-attached_storage

Procedure

The first step is to download the OSMC image to install it to our Raspberry Pi. Open the browser and navigate to the resource page below and download the disk image for your compatible Raspberry Pi model:

https://osmc.tv/download/

Raspberry Pi 2 / 3 / 3+

Release	Checksum (MD5)
2020.06-1	4e8deadf45442ee6fd242eb5baf3c4f1
2020.03-1	29f37713191b9047c441e44c900d7669
2020.01-1	e54ce9334355f645ff27b952f391008f
2019.11-1	294449f87b18e2f03ccfa885de30adac
2019.10-1	843c65cd48a21f7356207f9aca345c8a
2019.07-1	9db204483fd90621e0a3fa65a81a13a2
2019.06-1	3810303a48372d28853f83bacc3d34c4
2019.05-1	add3140ef75ccb5b76f118515d805af3
2019.04-1	3f98b076abe442629badc20a49cce885
2018.12-1	a995549a240a9b3bd195a5781e50b2e8
2018.10-1	9a04b9438a3bbef1c2cdcf78885bbf7a
2018.08-1	f69d8fb791311d13138ccb92c430f056
2018.07-1	a9627f0cfeade8b67006931a206e221b

Once you've downloaded the OSMC image, we can start to flash it on to the SD card. We shall not go over the process of flashing an image again. Refer to previous sections on how to do this with Ether, Raspberry Pi writer, etc.

Once you have flashed the image with OSMC image, boot the Raspberry Pi, which will bring up the installation window for KODI; wait until the process completes.

Next, select the language for the KODI installer, confirm your option, and proceed with the installation.

Next, set up the name for your KODI device. If you do not have other OSMC devices on your network, you can accept the default and proceed with the installation.

Next, the system will prompt you to enable or disable SSH for the Raspberry Pi. This step is optional, and you can work with the default.

The next step allows you to connect the device to a network. If you wish to connect to the Raspberry Pi to a network later, select the manual connection option and proceed.

Finally, set up the default options and finish the installation process.

The next step involves us adding media files to KODI's main space. Navigate to the side menu and select Files and click on add Videos. Doing this allows us to select the folder that KODI will scan and add media files to the library.

Select browse and add the directory that contains all your media files. Next, sort and organize the media files into various categories as prompted.

Finally, select okay, which will sort and add all your media files to the library. Kodi will search the names of the media from databases from the internet and add metadata information such as artists, posters, etc.

Raspberry Pi Torrenting With Deluge (Project #16)

In this project, we are going to set up a torrent seedbox using Raspberry Pi. A seedbox is a computer designed for downloading and uploading files using peer to peer network —commonly called torrents.

Although this is not an ideal seedbox, you can use it for both heavy and light torrenting services. For simplicity, we will not cover how to install and configure a VPN service on this project.

Requirements

Fully equipped Raspberry Pi – Monitor, Power supply, SD Card, etc

External Storage or NAS mounted storage devices

Internet connection

Procedure

As usual, the first step is to ensure the Raspberry Pi is fully updated using the apt command:

```
sudo apt-get update && sudo apt-get upgrade -y
```

For this project, we are going to use Deluge client for torrenting. You can also use other torrenting clients such as Transmission, QBitTorrent, etc.

NOTE: Ensure the torrent client you choose to use offers a web client that allows you to manage your torrents through your browser.

To install deluge and deluge web interface, enter the command:

```
sudo apt-get install deluged deluge-console deluge-web -y
```

Next, we need to set up a directory where we shall store all our torrent files for easy access. You should have read/write permissions for the directories.

Next, we need to start the deluged daemon to create the deluge configuration files. We will modify the configuration files to suit our needs. Use the command:

sudo deluged && sudo ps aux | pkill -i deluged

Next, we need to allow remote access by modifying the configuration file. Enter the command:

sudo deluge-console "config -s allow_remote True"

Once you've allowed remote access, we can create a user to access deluge, which you can do using the command:

sudo echo "<admin>:<123Password!>:10" >> ~/.config/deluge/auth

Make sure to replace admin and 123password! With the username and the password for the username, respectively.

With users and remote connection enabled, we need to restart deluge with the command deluged

Next, we can start the deluge web interface with the command

deluge-web -f

Open your browser and use the Raspberry Pi IP address followed by port 8112 to connect to the interface:

http://192.168.0.14:8112

Doing this will connect to the deluge-web interface —it will prompt you for a password. By default, the password is "deluge." You can modify the password later.

Once logged in, the operation will prompt you with a connection manager that displays all the available hosts. Select the required one and click connect. By default, it should be localhost followed by the deluge-daemon port: 127.0.0.1: 58846

Next, open preferences to set the download folder from the top bar.

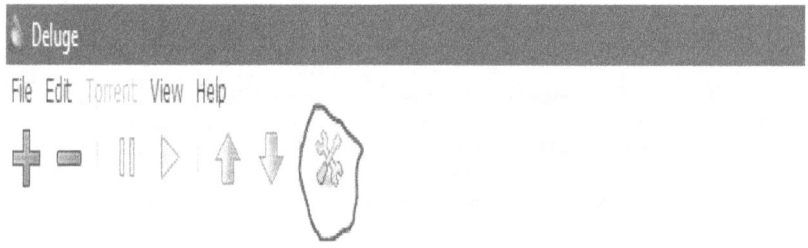

You can also update the password in the interface tab of the preferences. Next, enable the deluge service to start automatically on boot using the command:

sudo systemctl enable deluged.service

You can now start torrenting using your Raspberry Pi.

Raspberry Pi Google Assistant (Project #17)

In this project, we are going to turn our Raspberry Pi 4 into a Google Personal Assistant. The assistant works by listening to user voice command and performing the queries specified. You can activate it by saying, "Hey Google" or "Okay Google."

We will begin by setting up the audio, accessing the Google Assistant API, and then complete setting it up for full functionality.

Let us get started.

Requirements

Fully Equipped Raspberry Pi

Internet connection

Speakers

USB Microphone

Procedure

The first step we need to perform is to sign up for a Google Console account so that we access the Google Assistant code we need to use for the Raspberry Pi.

Open your browser, navigate to the following page, and create an account.

https://console.cloud.google.com/

After setting up your account successfully, open google actions from the URL below

https://console.actions.google.com/

Once in the Google Actions Dashboard, click create to initialize a new project.

Read and Agree to the Terms of Service as provided by Google and click Agree and continue.

Next, enter the project's name and set the country/region as well as the language of your preference.

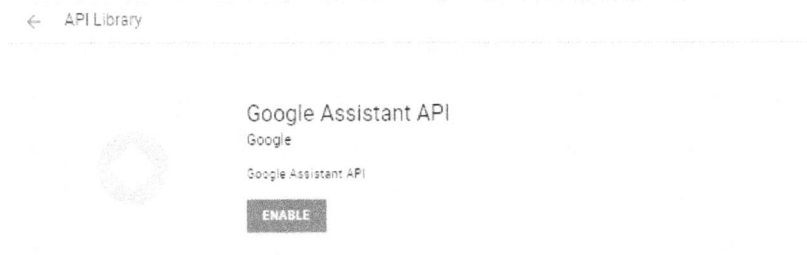

Next, navigate to Google Developers Console and enable Google Embedded Assitant API.

Navigate back to Google Actions Project page and select "Custom" and click Next. Search for the option "Are you looking to register and device?" and click on the link.

This action will take you to the Embedded device registration page. Click on the "Register model" option where you shall need to set the "Product Name," "Manufacturer," and "Device Type."

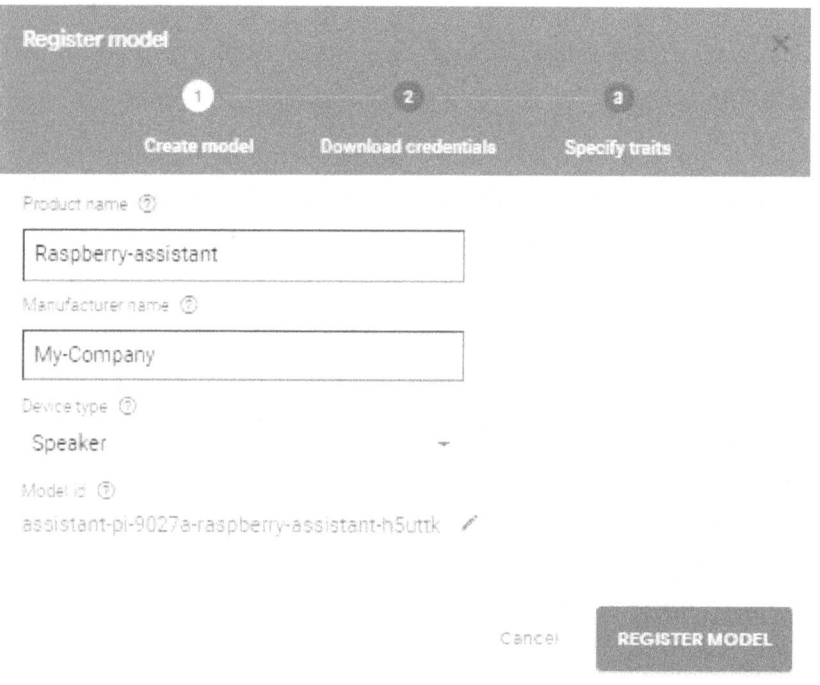

The three fields are necessary. You can fill any information for the first two. For the Device Type, select Speaker since we will set up a Google Assistant device.

NOTE: Make sure to note down the model-id; we will require it in upcoming steps, and then click "Register model."

The next step takes you to download credentials pane. The credentials are critical as we require them to allow the Raspberry to communicate with the server. Download the Credentials and save them on your computer.

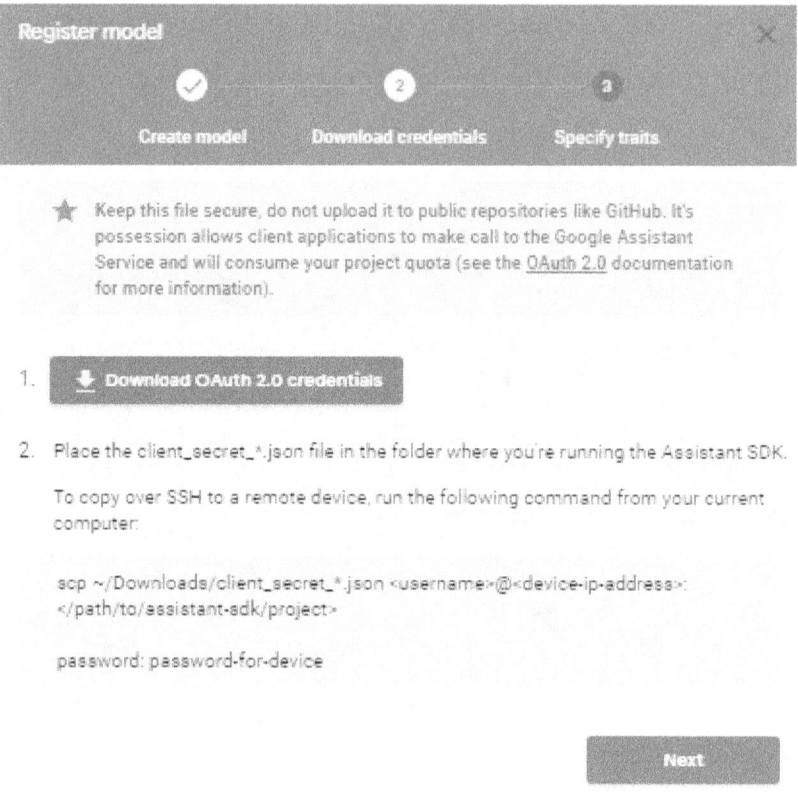

Next, select the traits or functionalities your device requires. You can choose any that matches your needs and then click Save Traits. Doing this should create a model that becomes available under Develop in "Device Registration."

The next step requires us to set up an OAuth Consent screen, which will allow us to authorize the Google Assistant later.

Open your browser and navigate to the page below and select the project we created in an earlier section —it should be on the top Menu.

https://console.developers.google.com/apis/credentials/consent

Next, under "User Type," select "External" and click Create.

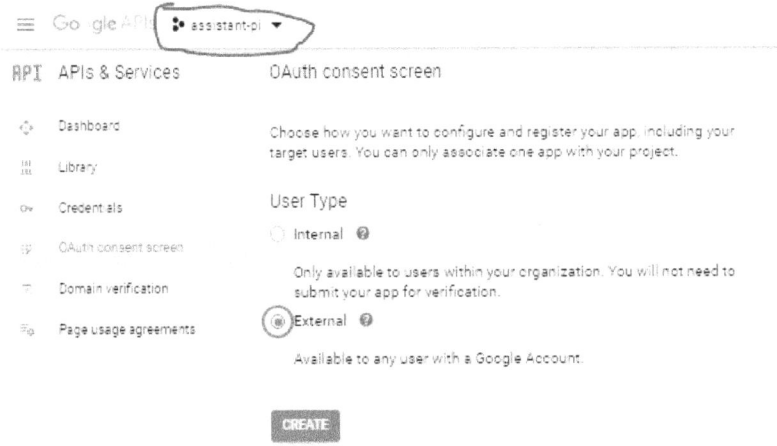

On the window that opens, fill the details accordingly. You can set the logo for the project, but that is not a requirement. Next, select the email to use and select save.

Next, to ensure that the Google Assistant works properly enable activities such as Location, Web and App Activity, Device Information, and Voice and Audio Activity in:

https://myactivity.google.com/activitycontrols

Next, ensure the Microphone and Speakers are working by trying a recording or play some media. We shall not go over how to test speakers.

Once we have finished setting up the Google Assistant API and hardware configured, we can start installing the Google Assistant SDK.

First, let us ensure that the Raspberry Pi is up to date with the command:

sudo apt-get update && sudo apt-get upgrade -y

Once fully updated, we can start installing all the requirements for Google Assistant.

First, create a directory and call it assistant-pi and then create a JSON configuration file with the commands:

sudo mkdir assistant-pi && cd assistant-pi && touch assistant-pi/config.json && nano config.json

In the config.json file we created, copy the contents of the JSON file we downloaded earlier and paste them. Save and close the file.

Next, we need to install Python and Python virtual environment with the command:

```
sudo apt install python3-dev python3-venv python3-pip libssl-dev libffi-dev libportaudio2
```

Next, enable the Python virtual environment using the command:

python3 -m assistant env.

Next, we need to install pip and setuptools with the command:

env/bin/python3 -m pip install --upgrade pip setuptools --upgrade

After that, we need to activate the virtual environment we created with the command

source /env/bin/activate

Now we can install The Google Assistant Library with the commands:

python3 -m pip install --upgrade google-assistant-library

python3 -m pip install --upgrade google-assistant-sdk[samples]

With all the requirements for running google assistant on our Raspberry Pi setup, we can start to authorize the system.

To do that, we start by installing the google authorization tool with the command:

python3 -m pip install --upgrade google-auth-oauthlib[tool]

Once we have the Google Authorization Library installed, we can run it, which generates an URL that you will use to auth it.

google-oauthlib-tool --client-secrets ~/googleassistant/credentials.json \

--scope https://www.googleapis.com/auth/assistant-sdk-prototype \

--scope https://www.googleapis.com/auth/gcm \

--save –headless

With the URL generated, copy it and open it on your browser, which should generate an authentication code. Copy this auth code and go back into the Terminal and paste it there.

Once the system accepts your authentication code, you will get a message indicating that you've successfully saved the credentials in the JSON file.

With everything configured, we need to execute the command below to allow google assistant to activate it.

googlesamples-assistant-pushtotalk --project-id <projectid>

Replace the project id with the id we copied earlier. Now you can talk to Google and perform various queries.

Finally, we need to set up google to activate without re-running the entire process. Enter the command:

googlesamples-assistant-pushtotalk

Google should respond to the "Okay Google" command. You can configure a custom hot word with the command

googlesamples-assistant-hotword

If the google assistant does not work, you may need to authorize your microphone and speakers.

Raspberry Pi FTP Server (Project #18)

In this project, we are going to set up a simple FTP server on the Raspberry Pi. Although FTP is an old technology that we can consider "outdated," it comes in handy when transferring files on local networks.

Requirements

Fully Equipped Raspberry Pi

Internet connection

Procedure

As usual, we will begin by updating our Raspberry Pi with the command:

```
sudo apt-get update && sudo apt-get upgrade -y
```

Next, we need to install FTP on our device using the command:

```
sudo apt-get install vsftpd -y
```

We now need to modify the FTP configuration file.

Open the file located under /etc/vsftpd.conf and enable the following options.

NOTE: Doing this requires you to remove the hashes at the beginning.

```
anonymous_enable=NO

local_enable=YES

write_enable=YES

local_umask=022

chroot_local_user=YES
```

Next, with the file opened, add the following lines:

```
user_sub_token=$USER

local_root=/home/$USER/ftp
```

Next, save the file and create an FTP directory for your current user. You can modify the permissions for the directory such that it becomes only accessible to the user. Next, restart the ftp service using the command:

systemctl restart vsftpd.service

Finally, get the IP address of your network interface and connect on port 21.

After that, the only thing left is to enter the username and password to connect to FTP.

Setting Up a Data Science Environment (project #19)

In this project, we are going to install a Python data science environment using Miniconda for arm architectures.

Requirements

Fully Equipped Raspberry Pi

Internet connection

Procedure

First, download the Miniconda installer for the Raspberry Pi from the continuum archive available here:

https://repo.anaconda.com/miniconda/

You can also use wget to download the file

```
Miniconda3-3.16.0-MacOSX-x86_64.sh      26.3M   2015-08-24 13:36:11   9t0t3167t413ddtae3dc36ebbbc8tat3
Miniconda3-3.16.0-Windows-x86.exe       38.5M   2015-08-24 13:38:07   5426c9046aea54e72d7f05f961249aaa
Miniconda3-3.16.0-Windows-x86_64.exe    41.2M   2015-08-24 13:38:13   4ae8fd63e4d9923fc45338c133a25b36
Miniconda3-latest-Linux-armv7l.sh       29.9M   2015-08-24 12:34:00   a01cbe457556576c2bb9833859cf9fd7
```

Next, set up the execute permissions on the file and run it with bash as:

chmod +x miniconda-*.sh && bash ./miniconda-*.sh

Finally, edit your bash profile file and add the following line:

export PATH="/home/pi/miniconda3/bin:$PATH"

Load the file by executing the command:

source .bashrc

That should do it:

Running a Flask Server On The Raspberry Pi (Project #20)

In this project, we are going to launch a simple flash project on our Raspberry Pi.

Flask is a web development framework for Python; it's more of a microframework with simple and lightweight functionality.

We shall not go over how flask works. You can learn that from reading the documentation available on the following resource page:

https://flask.palletsprojects.com/en/1.1.x/

Requirements

Fully Functional Raspberry Pi

Internet connection

Procedure

First, we need to ensure that we have Python installed and updated. Refer to the Python installation guide.

The next step is to install the Python flask package using pip. If you are using a version of Anaconda, use conda instead. You can refer to python modules from the official library here:

https://pypi.org/

pip3 install flask

Once Flask has completed installing, we can begin to create a web application project. Start by creating a directory for the project.

mkdir myProject && cd myProject

Once inside the directory, create a file called app.py and edit with your favorite text editor. vi app.py

Next, enter the following lines of code in the file

```python
from flask import Flask

app = Flask(__name__)

@app.route('/')
def index():
    return 'My First Flask App'

if __name__ == '__main__':
    app.run(debug=True, host='0.0.0.0')
```

Next, run the app with python3 app.py. This will start the server, which you can access by going to localhost:5000 to see the website:

#Bonus Project: Installing Kismet On the Raspberry Pi

This project shows you how to install Kismet on Raspberry Pi.

Kismet is a wireless network and device detector, sniffer, wardriving tool, and Wireless Intrusion Detection (WIDS) framework.

Check the official site for more information:

https://www.kismetwireless.net/

Requirements

Fully Equipped Raspberry Pi

Internet connection

Flashed firmware for Raspberry 3+

Procedure

Before using Kismet, we need to install hardware patches such as nexmon for Broadcom chips.

Start by updating and installing dependencies using the commands:

```
sudo apt-get update && sudo apt-get upgrade && sudo apt-get install git gawk qpdf adb flex bison
```

Next, open the browser and clone the nexmon repository to your directory of choice.

https://github.com/seemoo-lab/nexmon/

Navigate into the nexmon directory and start by installing i386 libraries.

```
sudo dpkg --add-architecture i386

sudo apt-get update

sudo apt-get install libc6:i386 libncurses5:i386 libstdc++6:i386
```

Next, set up the build-environment using the command:

source setup_env.sh.

NOTE: When executing the command, ensure that you're in the nexmon directory.

Compile the build tools and then extract flashpatches as well as the ucode from the original firmware files by executing the command:

make

Next, navigate to the patches folder of the raspberry pi's model. For example, raspberry 3+ is

bcm43455c0/7_45_154/

Next, compile a patched firmware with the make command.

Next, make a backup copy of your existing firmware with the command

```
make backup-firmware
```

Once done, install the patched firmware using the command

```
make install-firmware
```

Finally, we can install kismet with the commands.

```
wget                    -O                  -
https://www.kismetwireless.net/repos/kismet-
release.gpg.key | sudo apt-key add -

echo                                    'deb
https://www.kismetwireless.net/repos/apt/rele
ase/buster    buster    main'  |  sudo   tee
/etc/apt/sources.list.d/kismet.list

sudo apt update

sudo apt install kismet
```

You can now launch kismet and perform your network operations.

Conclusion

We have come to the end of the book.

We learned a lot about the Raspberry Pi and looked at cool projects you can create to have fun with your Pi 4.

Worth noting is that, because of updates, implementing some projects such as Google Assistant may change. In such instances, and should you run into issues, you can always check online resources to learn how to configure them; after all, learning through trial and error is the best kind of learning there is:

"The best way to prepare [to be a programmer] is to write programs and to study great programs that other people have written. In my case, I went to the garbage cans at the Computer Science Center, and I fished out listings of their operating systems."

Bill Gates

---

[1]   https://www.shutterstock.com/image-vector/raspberry-pi-top-view-illustration-260nw-1604969923.jpg

[2]   https://www.shutterstock.com/image-vector/raspberry-pi-top-view-illustration-260nw-1604969923.jpg

3   https://www.shutterstock.com/image-vector/raspberry-pi-top-view-illustration-260nw-1604969923.jpg

4   https://www.istockphoto.com/photo/black-ac-dc-power-supply-adapter-with-usb-connector-gm493724802-77056631

5   https://www.shutterstock.com/image-photo/closeup-raspberry-pi-board-connected-260nw-2531929773.jpg

6   https://www.istockphoto.com/photo/colorful-utp-ethernet-cables-lan-isolate-gm453568519-25736159?utm_medium=organic&utm_source=google&utm_campaign=iptcurl

7   https://www.shutterstock.com/image-photo/raspberry-pi-4-argon-one-260nw-2466901727.jpg

8   https://www.shutterstock.com/image-photo/ahmedabad-india-july-1st-2020-260nw-1767406739.jpg

9   https://www.istockphoto.com/photo/the-raspberry-pi-3-gm613319732-105863467?utm_medium=organic&utm_source=google&utm_campaign=iptcurl

10   https://img.freepik.com/premium-photo/woman39s-hand-typing-white-keyboard-with-red-letters-with-coffee-background-white-table_145713-1398.jpg

11   https://www.istockphoto.com/photo/dvi-hdmi-digital-video-cable-for-connecting-an-external-tv-screen-monitor-to-a-gm2159593146-

580171859?utm_medium=organic&utm_source=google&utm_campaign=iptcurl

12 https://img.freepik.com/premium-photo/hdmi-vga-adapter-cable-connector-computer-device_573652-2495.jpg

13 https://www.shutterstock.com/image-vector/isometric-set-audio-video-cable-600nw-1288957489.jpg

14 https://www.shutterstock.com/image-photo/hand-holding-blue-white-cable-network-2228818895?utm_campaign=image&utm_medium=googleimages&utm_source=iptc

15 https://www.istockphoto.com/video/macro-fingers-connect-cable-to-phone-with-open-microcircuit-gm1201116048-344314856?utm_medium=organic&utm_source=google&utm_campaign=iptcurl

16 https://www.shutterstock.com/image-photo/digital-camera-lens-ip-security-260nw-2126112242.jpg

17 https://encrypted-tbn0.gstatic.com/images?q=tbn:ANd9GcTYGXU3yM9hQ-6EQWL2q3nGTWZytl_eehFwig&s

18 https://www.shutterstock.com/image-photo/electrical-breadboard-connected-computer-closeup-260nw-436507327.jpg

19 https://www.shutterstock.com/image-photo/detail-electronic-cables-connector-isolated-260nw-2452163919.jpg

www.ingramcontent.com/pod-product-compliance
Lightning Source LLC
Chambersburg PA
CBHW072029230526
45466CB00020B/1159